THE GREER CASE

The Greer Case

* * * * *

A TRUE COURT DRAMA

* * * * *

BY

David W. Peck

CASSELL AND COMPANY LTD

London

CASSELL & CO LTD
37/38 St. Andrew's Hill, Queen Victoria Street
London, E.C.4

and at

31/34 George IV Bridge, Edinburgh; 210 Queen Street,
Melbourne; 26/30 Clarence Street, Sydney; 24 Wyndham
Street, Auckland, N.Z.; 1068 Broadview Avenue, Toronto 6;
P.O. Box 275, Cape Town; P.O. Box 11190, Johannesburg;
Munsoor Building, Main Street, Colombo 11; Haroon Cham-
bers, South Napier Road, Karachi; 13/14 Ajmeri Gate
Extension, New Delhi 1; 15 Graham Road, Ballard Estate,
Bombay 1; 17 Chittaranjan Avenue, Calcuta 13; Macdonald
House, Orchard Road, Singapore 9; Avenida 9 de Julho 1138,
São Paulo; Galeria Güemes, Escritorio 554/9, Florida 165,
Buenos Aires; P.O. Box 959, Accra, Gold Coast; 25 rue Henri
Barbusse, Paris 5e; 25 Ny Strandvej, Espergaerde, Denmark;
Kauwlaan 17, The Hague.

First published in Great Britain 1956

Printed in Great Britain by
Lowe and Brydone (Printers) Limited, London, N.W.10

CONTENTS

CONTENTS

ILLUSTRATIONS

PREFACE

WHEN *a judge writes a book that is not a lawbook an explanation is indicated. There is a double reason why I was moved to report the Greer case in book form.*

First, it satisfied my liking for mystery stories laid in a court setting. When the case on appeal came before the court over which I preside, I found that reading the record was not a legal chore but an absorbing reading experience. Here in truth was more drama, mystery and conflict, pathos, irony and even humour than one could dream up. The real-life characters—lawyers and witnesses, the woman who bore a son in poverty and obscurity, abandoned him, married into wealth and social prominence, spent her life half in fear and half in hope that her son would turn up, and died leaving a fortune to be sought in the search for her heir—were more interesting than characters that might be encountered in fiction.

Second, the case provided an excellent example of trial lawyers' work, of their problems in meeting a baffling case, of their resourcefulness, skill and untiring effort in discovering evidence, uncovering the truth and presenting a case in court. Their craftsmanship and creativeness, imagination and integ-

[ix]

rity, combined with the romance of the case, gave me both a professional pride and a personal pleasure in telling the story.

My conviction grew that this case should be reported in book form for general reading interest. At first I thought to suggest it to someone of literary talent. But I feared that such a person would be more inclined to take the frame for imaginative embellishment than to delve deeply into the record and exhibits to extract the natural flavour. This was not a case to inspire a story, I felt; it was the story.

It would have to be reduced, compacted and given the movement which court procedure retards. But the whole should be faithful to fact. The essential interest in the case lay in its actual ingredients of mystery, contest and personalities.

Thus the thought emerged that I might do the book. It was put off in the ever-continuing pressure of work. But it would not be denied. It reasserted itself from time to time, and finally demanded the recognition of holiday attention.

So here, one summer, in the hours between fishing Horse Creek and riding mountain trails, by coal-oil lamps at night, in a spare room kindly supplied by my host and referred to as the "Judge's study"; and here, another summer, between golf and bathing, in an appendage of a room atop a house known as the "Captain's Cabin," on the Siasconset bluff, I surrounded myself with the testimony and documents in the Greer case and have attempted to give you, with only due abbreviation, the story as the court heard it.

It is the story of the search and of the woman behind it, as it unfolded in the courtroom, as the witnesses told it, as the docu-

ments uncovered by the diligent digging of counsel disclosed it. It is also a story of lawyers matching wits for a high stake, of their ingenuity and assiduity, and of what goes on behind the scenes of a court drama.

DAVID W. PECK

T-Cross Ranch
Dubois, Wyoming, 1952

Siasconset, Massachusetts, 1954

The Greer Case

Mrs. Greer—Lady with a Past

* * * * *

O N THE morning of August 11, 1946, the obituary page
of New York newspapers reported the death of Mabel
Seymour Greer. It was an announcement befitting the passing
of a member of the "400", formal in text, nostalgic in tone. Ap-
propriate note was made of her social prominence and charita-
ble activities and of the fact that, leaving no children or relatives, she had willed her fortune to Harvard University, her
husband's alma mater and principal beneficiary under his own
will. There was only a suggestion of the stir created in society
forty years before when she had married the scion of one of
America's first families. There was no hint that the ending of her
life was to be the beginning of a great court battle over her will
and wealth, testing the talent and tenacity of an array of lawyers and absorbing the public in the daily reporting of the trial.

Louis Morris Greer had only just preceded his wife in death.
They had reached the quiet years and had retired from a social
world of which they had so long been a vital part. More accurately, perhaps, that world had retired with them—the era of

elegance, of Fifth Avenue mansions and their counterparts in the estates that stretched in expansive lawn to the sea at Newport and Long Island, crowned the bluff of Bar Harbor and spread over the rolling Berkshire Hills. That era had flowered in the economic and social climate of the years between the turn of the century and the outbreak of the First World War. It survived for another generation but ebbed away as the Second World War permanently changed the world.

The Greers changed too. They moved to an apartment. He centered his interest in business; she devoted herself to charity. Members of the present generation remember him as a leader in the realm of finance, an executive of the giant utility company which supplies the City of New York with gas and electricity. They remember her as a large-bosomed, white-haired woman, the image of Queen Victoria.

An older generation remembered him as the exemplar of the elegant age, one to the manner born, a great-grandson of Robert Morris, signatory of the Declaration of Independence. They remembered him on the Avenue, with his high hat, neat dress, and walking stick. It was on such an occasion in the spring of 1908, according to reports, that he indulged a natural gallantry and rescued two lovely ladies from the distress of a carriage drawn to the curb with a broken wheel and invited them to Sherry's for tea. One of the ladies was Mabel Seymour.

She was remembered by those who attended the fashionable wedding that autumn as the girl who came from nowhere and snatched the prize. Those who were willing to do her justice admired what they saw—a perfectly proportioned figure, with a promise of distinction, a cherubic face lighted by large liquid eyes and etched only by a cleft of the upper lip and dimple in the chin, alabaster skin, and the crowning glory of a profusion of chestnut hair in a regal coil.

What Louis Greer learned of her lineage beyond what was stated in their application for a marriage licence is not known. A soft English accent confirmed a stated English birth. One would not have been inclined at the time to question her age, stated as twenty-seven, or that she was twelve years her husband's junior. Just before she went to live on Fifth Avenue and Long Island as Mrs. Greer, she had resided at the Hotel Seymour, an estimable establishment on Forty-fourth Street. In the years between her marriage and death, she enjoyed all the luxury of the times, the elegance of the prewar years, the prosperity of the postwar years. She had wealth and social position. She had friends, but in the circle in which she moved no one had known her prior to 1908.

Few who read the death notice that August morning of 1946 had read or recalled another death notice seven years earlier, and none perceived any connection between the two. Although also reported in a New York paper, it was a different set of people, cities apart, who found interest in the report of the death of Dr. Willard B. Segur of Ware, Massachusetts, on January 28, 1939. It stated that Dr. Segur, aged 73, had been born in Ohio, graduated from Princeton University in 1889 and from the Dartmouth Medical School in 1892, for forty-two years had practised medicine in Ware and the neighbouring town of Enfield and had long been medical examiner of the district. He left surviving him his widow, a son and an adopted son, Harold A. Segur of Worcester.

Unconnected as the lives and deaths so reported seemed to be, they were vividly linked in further newspaper reports of quite different character within one month after Mrs. Greer's death. The newspapers then reported that, just before her death, Mrs. Greer had acknowledged that an illegitimate son

B   [5]

had been born to her and Dr. Segur, when they both were very young, and that Dr. Segur had adopted the child. This startling disclosure was made by Mrs. Greer's lawyer in a statement which accompanied the filing of her will.

The newspapers soon followed with the announcement that Dr. Segur's adopted son, Harold A. Segur, had brought legal action to upset Mrs. Greer's will and claim inheritance of her fortune. The executor of her estate conceded that she had borne a son by Dr. Segur but contested the claim of Harold Segur that he was the son.

Thus the lines of legal battle were drawn. The trial that ensued was headline news for many a day. Lawyers far and wide followed the case with the utmost interest. Bankers, brokers and businessmen at their breakfast tables, typists at their desks, society matrons at leisure and housewives between household chores read with quickening interest the daily developments of the case. All and sundry were caught up in the contest and the chase, the baffling puzzle and developing drama, as the wheels of justice ground slowly but exceeding fine.

Court Convenes

* * * * *

THE blue-uniformed figure who preceded the black-robed figure was himself a personification of the law. For forty years he had been making this entrance, through the panelled door behind the bench, and allowing a measured moment for the judge to take his place beside the high chair, pronouncing the chant of the court crier:

Hear ye, hear ye, all persons having business with this Surrogate's Court of the County of New York, draw near, give your attendance and you shall be heard.

The cry was always finished before the final stroke of ten. Every day was the same in the ritual, the formality with which court was convened. Impersonal as was the call to order, unvaried the inflection of the chant, concealed the personal pride of the officer in his ancient function, there was meaning in the erect figure, steady look and even tone. It was as if to say, "This day begins, this day be done, in the endless search for truth, the eternal quest for justice."

This twenty-first day of April 1947 was no different from any other day, except for the case that would be called. It was another day in the hundred and fifty years the Surrogate's Court had been administering deceased persons' estates. Another day in guarding the interests of widows, protecting the rights of children, examining the accounts of executors and trustees, hearing will contests and resolving conflicting claims to the property of the dead.

The Honourable James A. Delehanty, Surrogate, took his seat on the bench and for the several thousandth time surveyed the familiar scene of court attendants, like sentinels, posted at the ends and entrance of the great room, lawyers at the counsel table below the bench, and, beyond the railing which enclosed the lawyers' preserve, the rows of interested parties, witnesses and spectators. He beheld the courtroom, and the eyes looked beyond the transient to the traditional.

The people changed case by case. His own occupancy of the high place was only less temporary. But the courtroom was the embodiment of the everlasting, fittingly built with nobility of design by unhurried artisans who knew that their legacy was the timeless temple of justice.

The quiet here was not to be disturbed by the roar of traffic rolling down from Brooklyn Bridge or along the streets which converge into City Hall Park and the bottleneck of lower New York. The clatter of that outer world was shut out by the massive stone of the walls, as the light slanting in from the high windows was screened by drapes of deep red velvet.

Rising two stories from the red velour carpet to the gold-leaf ceiling, crisscrossed by heavy beams with carved rosettes, the room was panelled in rich-grained mahogany, crowned at the cornice with decorative carvings of books, figures and insignia of the law. Embossed on the doors were the scales of justice resting on the point of the sword of righteousness. Anyone within was thus reminded at a glance of the business of his errand.

The Honourable James A. Delehanty, venerable and white-haired, looked and lived his part. Learned in the law, searching in mind, nothing escaped his discernment. As the capacious ear heard the testimony, the practised eye observed the witnesses. Both the hearing and seeing were recorded in a retentive memory. His reactions were not registered, however, in any wrinkling of the high, round forehead, twinkling of the quiet grey eyes, or expression of the smooth, pale face. If the impression given was one of coldness, it was not one of indifference. He cared. He cared for the right and the truth and meant to find them; nothing else mattered.

At his nod, the court clerk rose from his seat immediately below the bench and called the case of "Matter of Mabel Seymour Greer."

"Counsel will please note their appearances for the Court," he said.

Lester Friedman was quick to respond. From his place on claimant's side of the counsel table he rose and said, "If your Honour please, I represent the claimant, Harold A. Segur. We are ready to proceed."

The stocky contender was ready. He had spent long days for many weeks in locating and interviewing witnesses, in order to bring them to this place on this day to support the claim of his client that he was the son of Mabel Seymour Greer and entitled to contest her will and inherit her estate.

The weeks of work had been without compensation, and the arduous trial days ahead would be without compensation, unless the lawyer's efforts should be crowned with success. Segur had no money to pay a lawyer. Indeed, he had told a newspaper reporter in an interview at his home in Worcester before the start of the case, "To be frank with you, I don't even have the money to afford the trip or trips to New York that a court proceeding of this kind would entail, much less the lawyers' fees. I never had any business with lawyers."

Fortunately, however, it was possible for Segur to retain a lawyer who would take the case on a contingent basis, and let the payment of any fee and the amount depend on winning a sum of money out of which the fee could be paid. Although many lawyers will not take a case without payment of a fixed fee or the assurance of payment for their time by a financially responsible client, most lawyers will take a chance with a client who has a promising case. This entirely proper professional arrangement, which enables a poor man with an honest claim to secure legal representation, served Segur very well. Although unable to pay in advance or to commit himself to pay any certain amount, Segur could obtain highly competent counsel on a contingent basis, because he had a huge stake in the Greer estate—a possible right to half a million dollars—enough to pay a successful lawyer handsomely and to live on Easy Street himself the rest of his life.

This was more money than Segur had ever dreamed of possessing, until one day, just a few months earlier, the mystery of a lifetime had been cleared up when he received the strange and surprising news that a woman whose name and very existence were unknown to him was his mother and that she had died leaving a fortune. Unfortunately she had not bequeathed the money to her son, so it was not simply there to be collected. On the contrary, she had willed almost her entire fortune to Harvard University and had disinherited the child, so that he could come into his own only by successfully waging a will contest.

Segur had two grounds of attack. One, a woman could not

under law disinherit a child and leave more than half her property to charity. A child had a legal right to take half the estate. Two, this will might be upset on the ground that when it was made, during the last days of Mrs. Greer's life, she was not in full possession of her faculties and thus not competent to make a will. Segur had been advised that there was a good chance of invalidating the will on that ground, and in that event a surviving child would be entitled to take the entire estate. Therefore, if he could establish himself as Mrs. Greer's son, he would be entitled to inherit half of her property and perhaps all of it.

Thus Harold A. Segur was in court to press his claim of kinship to Mrs. Greer and to attack her will. But one thing at a time, the judge had ruled. First, Segur would have to prove that he was Mrs. Greer's son. Was he? That was the question of the day.

Segur was fortunate in his counsel. Lester Friedman had a solid reputation as a lawyer and was as sturdy of mind as of body, and equally stout of heart. His dark eyes flashed his fervour, and a firm jaw pronounced his determination. Here and now he had a case worthy of his mettle, a cause as well as a stake worth fighting for. And he believed in his case, that Harold Segur was the illegitimate son of Mabel Seymour Greer, with all the rights of a child.

Armbruster believed it too, Friedman thought as he sat waiting for the opening of court and the call of his case that morning. But Armbruster sat across the table in opposition.

Raymond Armbruster had his own thoughts. He was pensive, had been pensive about the Greer case for a long time. He had a dual responsibility. As the draftsman of Mrs. Greer's will and attorney for the Fifth Avenue Bank, the executor under the will, he had a duty to sustain the will and the bequests she had made. He likewise had a duty to disclose any information he

[11]

possessed as to any possible heirs and to see that the estate he represented was distributed according to law.

Armbruster knew that he was going to be embarrassed in this case. His own statement to the court, when he filed the will, disclosing the existence of a child and indicating that Harold A. Segur was that child, had been the start of the case. Now he was opposing Segur and would be a witness against him. But Armbruster had no uneasiness of conscience. He had the duty to be honest, not to guess right. Had not the newspapers that very morning suggested that the solution of the puzzle would require the combined talents of a Hercule Poirot, Clarence Darrow and Justice Oliver Wendell Holmes?

He did not pretend to that insight. It was sufficient for him to state the facts, as he knew them, whenever called upon, and he would continue to do so. As his own testimony would be an important part of the case, he had wisely decided not to act as trial counsel for the executor and had retained the eminent firm of Coudert Brothers for this purpose. It was Francis D. Wells of that firm who sat at the head of the counsel table on the defending side and who rose in his turn to announce his appearance for the executor in opposition to Segur.

Wells was up to the responsibility. Though he was still under forty, greying at the temples had started to mark a finely chiselled face with distinction. He had been well schooled in the law and well trained in practice according to the exacting standards of a great firm, which had recognized and rewarded his ability and diligence with a partnership. Pleasant of manner and voice, he eschewed histrionics and relied on meticulous preparation and matter-of-fact presentation. Painstaking study of all the information at hand about Mrs. Greer and Harold Segur had left him puzzled and unsatisfied. He wanted to know more. But he thought that the known facts fell short of establishing Segur's claim, and he would constantly remind the court that the burden of proof was on his adversary.

A third appearance was made by a lean, thoughtful-looking person seated also on the opposite side of the table from Friedman, behind Wells and Armbruster. A familiar figure in the Surrogate's Court, he did not have to announce himself. For fifteen years, as counsel to the Public Administratur of New York County, Joseph A. Cox had been in court nearly every day. In his soft-spoken but never diffident way, he told the court of the Public Administrator's interest in the case and that the state might have a claim to Mrs. Greer's estate.

The Public Administrator is a public official charged with the responsibility of administering the estates of persons who die without leaving a valid will and without readily identifiable relatives. Also, if there is no relative closer than a cousin, the Public Administrator may challenge and contest the validity of a will, either on the ground that the person making the will was not competent at the time or was under another's undue influence. If the attack is successful and there are no relatives to inherit, the state takes the property. This is an ancient prerogative of governments.

All right and standing of the Public Administrator to challenge the validity of Mrs. Greer's will depended on defeating the claim of Segur. If Segur could establish himself as Mrs. Greer's son, all right of attack on the will and of inheritance resided in him, and the Public Administrator would be completely out. On the other hand, if Segur should be unsuccessful in establishing his claim, the Public Administrator was entitled to contest the will, and in the event of success and no other claimant's turning up and proving himself, the state would inherit. Therefore, the Public Administrator was very much interested in the lawsuit that was getting under way and in its outcome.

His counsel, Mr. Cox, had a further and more personal interest. The Public Administrator of New York County is a salaried official. His counsel, on the other hand, works on a fee basis. He is remunerated from the assets of the estates in which he is involved, in an amount fixed by the court, in accordance with his contribution to the proper administration of the estates. Obviously, if his only contribution to the Greer estate should be unsuccessful opposition to the true heir, he would not be entitled to much of an allowance. But if he were instrumental in saving the estate from an unfounded claim, or in successfully waging a will contest on his own, or even in discovering an heir, his contribution would be substantial and his compensation correspondingly large.

Cox was of the opinion that Mrs. Greer had not been competent when she made her will. To that extent he was in agreement with Segur. But the validity of the will was not the issue at this time. The question was whether Harold Segur was Mrs. Greer's son with all the rights flowing therefrom. On that issue Cox was as opposed to Segur as was Wells. Thus for different reasons and with different interests Cox and Wells were siding together to defeat Segur.

Each of the three trial lawyers was committed to his own objective, strategy and tactics. Each had deeply laid plans, carefully calculated on the basis of his knowledge of the case and his contemplation of how it would develop. But each was sure that he was in for surprises, because the one thing of which all were certain was that no one knew all there was to know about the case, Mrs. Greer, Dr. Segur, Harold Segur or, perhaps, about other important though as yet unknown figures. Despite all plans, therefore, there would likely be occasions for improvisation.

One thing the attorneys had in common, which would largely dictate and control all tactics and procedure, was the judge who would preside. The case was to be tried before a judge without a jury, and this meant that they would be spared a lot of preliminaries and educational excursions for the benefit of jurors. It meant also that they would have to forgo some of the excesses, sentimental appeals and little devices which might be calculated to sway a jury but which would be repulsed or resented by a trained and emotionally disciplined judge.

The pattern of a trial may vary in accordance with the known capacity, understanding and idiosyncrasies of a particular judge. All the lawyers in this case knew that Judge Delehanty, although reserved, would be the dominant factor, the pattern-maker and pacemaker. He was an inexorable and impersonal logician who discouraged all distractions from a single-minded pursuit of the truth. Some judges generate a warm and cozy atmosphere in a courtroom and even stimulate exchanges of wit. Surrogate Delehanty did not. He was an aloof and impenetrable judge, but he was exceedingly able, upright and fair, and lawyers had the highest regard for him and instinctively met his standards.

Therefore, this case would be tried with much less embroidery than a jury case and with fewer trimmings than even most nonjury cases. This was made clear at the outset by the Surrogate's invitation to Lester Friedman to open the case in behalf of the claimant.

"Do you wish to make an opening statement, Mr. Friedman?" the judge inquired. "You can be quite brief, as I am generally familiar with the case."

Opening Statement

• • • • •

"IF YOUR Honour please," Friedman began, "Mabel Seymour Greer died in this city on August 10, 1946, leaving an estate of over $500,000, most of which she left to charity by a will which my learned friend, Mr. Armbruster, has offered for probate. The only assumption upon which this will can stand is that Mrs. Greer left no child. Such an assumption is false." A ringing tone was already developing in a naturally high-pitched voice.

"Mrs. Greer left a son. Not a publicly acknowledged son, because the son was not Mr. Greer's. Indeed, Mrs. Greer was at pains all during her married life to keep her secret from her husband. Nevertheless, she confided to a number of people, her household retainers and friends, that she had a child when she was a young girl and that the child was living. She described that child as having been born to her in Boston, the offspring of a liaison with a college student taking premedical courses, named Willard B. Segur, who became a prominent doctor and adopted the child. That child, the adopted son of Dr. Segur, is here this day to claim his rightful inheritance."

So plainly stated, with dramatic assurance, the claim of Harold A. Segur was set forth.

The Surrogate was not prone to let positiveness impress him. He would question a lawyer starting off too confidently on an obstacle course. He raised the first hurdle, a piece of paper which lay on the bench before him.

Holding it up for Friedman's attention, he said, "By this paper, sir, your client has waived all claim to the Greer estate. What do you say to that?"

The lawyer was not to be daunted. "I am glad your Honour mentioned that. It is not a reflection on my client's claim." A calculated emphasis on "my" and a cold glance at Armbruster punctuated the statement.

"When Mr. Segur is given the opportunity of taking the witness stand, he will explain to your Honour the circumstances under which he was prevailed upon to sign that paper. In short, it was the assurance of being spared the publicity which this case has visited upon him and his family. The assurance failed, and I am confident that your Honour will relieve him from the stipulation.

"And now, if I may continue—and I will be very brief, for your Honour would not want me to narrate all the testimony in advance—the evidence will establish beyond question that Mrs. Greer had a son by Dr. Segur, and I think we will be able to establish to your satisfaction that Harold Segur is that child.

"While we cannot rest on the report made to the Court by Mr. Armbruster when he filed the will"—again the speaker looked across the table but did not catch the eyes that seemed far away—"Mr. Armbruster did make an investigation to ascertain whether Mrs. Greer left any heirs, and with your Honour's permission I will read what Mr. Armbruster reported to this court at that time.

[17]

"This is his affidavit." The emphasis this time was on the "his".

The lawyer then read from his adversary's statement—that Armbruster had been told by Mrs. Greer of the birth of a child out of wedlock in Boston and that the child had been adopted by his father, Willard B. Segur; that, to ascertain the identity and whereabouts of the child, he had interviewed former employees and friends of Mrs. Greer who had confirmed the fact that Mrs. Greer had told them that when she was a very young girl she had a son by Dr. Segur, and that Dr. Segur had adopted the child.

The affidavit continued to the effect that Armbruster had gone to Worcester, Massachusetts, and had there located Harold A. Segur, the adopted child of Dr. Segur, and concluded with this statement:

I feel that Harold A. Segur is Mrs. Greer's son and is the person of whom she spoke, but I am not definitely certain of this fact nor do I have any documentary evidence to prove it. I thoroughly believe, from the investigations I have made, that Mrs. Greer had no living relatives other than the son of whom she spoke to me and to other people.

Letting the document which he had drawn from the court files drop on the table, Friedman lifted his eyes and voice.

"That is what Mr. Armbruster thought until someone suggested that Harvard University could use the money better than Mr. Segur. We have no complaint that we are put to our proof. We can and will prove that Harold Segur is Mrs. Greer's son. And now, if your Honour please, I will call our first witness, Mrs. Annie Jackson, who was Mrs. Greer's maid for twenty-five years."

Fighting for an Inheritance

* * * * *

AS Harold Segur sat there in the front row, listening to his lawyer's opening statement, what he heard and saw hardly seemed to concern him. So quiet, so unobtrusive had his whole life been that he felt out of place as the centre of the legal battle which was just beginning, and he dreaded the day. Despite his determination to fight for his inheritance, he shied away from it and slumped rather than straightened as his lawyer asserted his claim. It was consciousness of his paunch rather than anything he heard which brought him up. The silver-rimmed spectacles that lined the grey hair were supposed to make the vision clear. But everything was too confusing. He took them off and let them dangle from his hand.

What he then saw was not a courtroom or pyramid of figures to a judicial apex. It was the long stretch of his life leading to the parlour of that second-floor apartment on Auburn Street, Worcester. Sixty years he knew it covered, although he had no birth certificate to mark the start. He saw at the beginning that boarding house in Boston, with nothing but women around, and his mother who was not his mother. He saw a hospital and a handsome man in white whom this woman took him to visit. Then one day they moved out of the boarding house and went to live with the doctor in the little town of Enfield. Dr. Segur then became "Dad" to him.

School days started at the same time. There were a succession of schools: public school, private school, finally Dartmouth. All the learning—all the learning—except who he was. That he never learned. That Mary O'Donnell, who had raised him and had become Mary Segur, was not his mother, he knew. But for the doctor he had the feeling of a son—so much so that when the day came in 1907 when Mary Segur left the doctor's house, he had no hesitancy in choosing to stay with the doctor.

He had never seen Mary Segur again until her death twenty years later. It was only then that he gave up the quest for his parentage. On that point the doctor also had been silent as the tomb. Only once had he permitted the slightest suggestion to cross his lips. Only after being told of the boy's decision to stay with him when his wife, the boy's foster mother, left, had he said, "I am glad, and you are right. Always remember that blood is thicker than water."

Then another twenty years later came Armbruster. First his long-distance call and the mysterious questions: Had he ever heard of Mrs. Greer? Had he ever been to Long Island? That much at least was easy to answer. No. Then the request to see him, and the words coming from afar, out of another world, dumfounding: "I can prove that Dr. Segur was your father."

And the next day Armbruster called in person. There in the parlour, surrounded with the photographs of his four sons, and the likeness of Dr. Segur looking down from the mantel, he heard the news of his birth. Dr. Segur was his father. Mrs.

Greer was his mother. She had not remembered him in her will because she felt that the doctor had made ample provision for him. That was a joke. But he had the right to contest Mrs. Greer's will and claim her estate. However, he was told that would take years of time, would involve large expense and in the end he might not succeed, having caused only publicity and notoriety to himself and his family. But if he would sign a waiver of any claim, there would be no publicity.

He had half turned away from Armbruster and had looked long into the eyes looking down from the mantel, as his mind searched for the answer to the new perplexity. Was this then the end of the road—or the beginning? At last, in this strange fashion, he knew who he was—and now should he proclaim it, advertise it, and with new pains and burdens enter on a chase for a pot of gold at a rainbow's end, or should he let the grave hold its secret and his? The dead did not answer.

But the living did. In the faces of his four sons, in thoughts of his wife, the answer was clear and decisive. The family had little of worldly goods, but they had built in quiet respectability by earnest effort the good home and good name of the family. So much more precious this than riches, that no price was worth exhuming the past and forgotten.

Armbruster was prepared. Segur was prepared. Never more proudly had he signed his name—his name—than to the paper Armbruster handed across the table.

Then it all broke. The blaring headlines in New York and Worcester papers, screaming into his soul all the merciless publicity he was to have been spared, violating all that his love and care and sacrifice were to make inviolate.

Oh, it had all been explained, satisfactorily in a way. It was not Armbruster's fault. He had tried to avoid the publicity but

c

had to disclose the facts to the court in connection with the presenting of the will, and somehow a reporter had got on the trail, and all pains for privacy had gone for naught.

So Segur was here—at least now with full justification and no little determination. The press clipping he carried in his pocket was his own facing of the world. As he had said to the reporter:

> Now that all this has become public, I have every intention of fighting for and obtaining for myself what is justly and legally due. Besides, I have a family of my own to think about. Up to now it was the thought of my wife and four grown boys that prevented me from coming out into the open and proclaiming myself the illegitimate son of Mrs. Greer. Now that the whole world knows it, I will have no hesitation in claiming the inheritance that is due me.

5

Annie Jackson—As the Maid
Told the Story

* * * * *

A TIMID smile and a timid step were her response to the
call of her name. Although she had been subjected to
many interviews by different lawyers, each trying to get a different meaning out of the same facts, she was still not used to
their ways or comfortable about going through it all again for a
lot of strangers.

Annie Jackson's place was in the home, and the good servant
listened rather than talked. Her bland face and plain dress indicated that confidences would be well kept. The household had
its confidences which accompanied the daily tasks. The relation
between a lady and her maid was a close one. Too bad, after the
long quiet years of service, and now the quieter years of retire-
ment on a remembrance, that others had to pry.

But she understood. Where there was money, people would
gather. And that nice man, Harold Segur—it wasn't his fault
that he was here, either—was right in seeking his inheritance
if he was poor Mrs. Greer's son. Anyway, what could she do but

tell once more what Mrs. Greer had told her, just as she remembered it?

The judge was very businesslike. A gesture toward the chair up front beside him brought her forward, and there she sat facing some familiar faces in a very unfamiliar setting.

Friedman's questioning was as homely as he could make it. "Mrs. Jackson, how long did you know Mrs. Greer?" he began.

"I was with—you want to know how long I was with Mrs. Greer?" The witness repeated the question, as if to herself, to gain a second to collect her thoughts. Then precisely and quietly came the answer: "Twenty-four years and seven months."

"You can speak a little louder, please, Mrs. Jackson." The lawyer wanted to accustom the witness to her surroundings and place her on a proper level of communication with her auditors. He repeated the answer in full voice, though in question form. "Twenty-four years and seven months you were in her employ?"

Yes, that was the time, and in that time the servant was on unusually intimate terms with her mistress, accompanying her when she went driving, and staying with her when she visited her home in Bayville, Long Island.

"Did Mrs. Greer confide in you?" the lawyer asked.

"She did," the witness acknowledged.

"Did Mrs. Greer ever tell you about her son?"

"She did."

"When for the first time did she speak to you about her son?"

"After I was with her about ten years she began to tell me about her son."

"Tell us what she said to you about her son at that time?"

Mrs. Jackson had been carefully led to the point and now picked up the thread in her own words.

"She said to me that she had something she would like to tell me, providing I didn't mention it for it to harm her. That was the way she began. Then she said to me that she had—this child had been born to her in her younger age and that the child had been left where it was born, in the house where it was born and she had never returned to see it, and then she went on with the story—how she had wanted to see the child—and I listened to her story very carefully and I tried to lighten her burden by saying that she didn't do the worst thing in the world—and I said, 'Why didn't you ever return to see about it?' and then she said that she had no money. She wanted to do something for the child, but after she had married Mr. Greer she could not afford to have him find out, and that was the burden that she had been carrying all the years."

"Did she tell you where it was that the child was born?" the lawyer resumed.

"Well, she said in a boarding house in Boston."

"Did she ever tell you who the father of the child was?"

"That Dr. Segur was the father of the boy."

"Did she ever tell you about the fact that the boy had been adopted?"

"Yes. In 1939, when this doctor died and she saw the death notice in the paper, she came into the kitchen and said to me— she read it to me while I was getting the dinner—and when she got to the part about his leaving an adopted son, she said, 'That's my boy.'"

"You are talking now about the death notice of Dr. Willard Segur?"

"Yes. And that was the time that she said, 'I thought that he would adopt it and I am happy that he did.'"

"After she had first spoken to you about her son, how often did Mrs. Greer speak to you about her son?"

"Well, that was almost every day she would say something after the first."

"Now, Mrs. Jackson—" a slight change of tone by the examiner indicated a shift in the course of the examination— "on June 3, 1946, did you admit Mr. Raymond T. Armbruster, the attorney, to Mrs. Greer's apartment?"

"Yes."

"After Mr. Armbruster left did Mrs. Greer tell you about her conference with Mr. Armbruster?"

"Yes."

"What did she tell you?"

"She said—in fact I knew before he came what it was all about. She said, 'I was talking to Mr. Armbruster, as you know, about making my will,' and he had advised her not to leave the boy anything. That was the way she put it."

Satisfied with this simple, straightforward presentation of his first witness, Friedman sat down. Before him on the table lay a photograph. The enigmatic beauty of the face caught him once more. He had looked again and again, long and searchingly, into that portrait, trying to fathom the subject's character and gain insight into her riddle. Even now he was lost for the moment in the contemplation. Without betraying the mental drift, he lifted himself, saying, "One thing more, your Honour. May I ask Mrs. Jackson if she can identify the lady in this photograph?"

The witness took the photograph and replied, "Yes. That is Mrs. Greer in her wedding dress."

Wells admired the brevity and simplicity of Friedman's presentation. It was well calculated to make the case seem A, B, C. A logical sequence—Mrs. Greer had a son, the son was adopted by Dr. Segur, Harold Segur was Dr. Segur's adopted son, therefore Harold Segur was Mrs. Greer's son. His job was to destroy the simplicity and wreck the conclusion.

With the premise that Mrs. Greer had a son, he would not quarrel. He was satisfied on that score. Also, assuredly, Harold

Mrs. Greer as a bride

Segur was the adopted son of Dr. Segur, and Mrs. Greer may well have thought that the adopted son was her son. But Wells was convinced that the wish was father to the thought, and the premise which he would attack was the supposition that the adopted son was the same as Mrs. Greer's son. He lost no time in going to the attack.

"Do you recall that incident in 1939 of Mrs. Greer coming into the kitchen to see you?" he asked.

"I do," the witness replied.

"Did Mrs. Greer have anything in her hands at that time?"

"Nothing but a newspaper."

"Did you see the paper?"

"I never noticed it, because I was in the midst of my dinner, very busy, and she simply sat on the chair and was reading the article to me. I never stopped my work."

"Was Mrs. Greer excited at the time?"

"Very excited, very nervous."

"Tell me exactly what she told you after she read it to you, Annie?" Wells's tone was confidential.

The witness was as exact as memory would permit.

"She read the death notice in the paper and when she had gotten to the part that she wanted me to get, about him having an adopted son, she said to me, 'I am so happy, now that I know that the boy is alive and has been properly taken care of, and his father adopted him.'"

"Did she make any other statement at that point?" the lawyer inquired.

"Well, at that time I began to turn around. If I can recall readily I was at the stove fixing something, and I said to her, 'Well, that should make you happy.'"

"No," Wells corrected, "I am not asking you what you told Mrs. Greer. I am asking you to tell me from your best recollection what Mrs. Greer told you. Was there anything else that she said to you at that time, Annie?"

"I can't . . . As I said . . ."

Wells had sympathy for the woman's confusion. He did not wish or need to confuse her. Interrupting, he took the lead.

"On your direct examination by Mr. Friedman, I believe you said that Mrs. Greer told you, 'That's my boy.' Is that right?"

"Yes; yes."

"But when I examined you sometime ago, on a pretrial examination, you testified that Mrs. Greer had said, 'That *must be* my boy.' Isn't that so, Annie?"

"Yes," the witness obliged.

"Yes," Wells reiterated. "Let me read your answer then."

Picking up the transcript of the previous testimony, he read: "I think when the father died she saw it in the evening newspaper and the paper read about how this doctor had left a wife and one son and an adopted son, and she brought the paper and showed it to me and she said, 'This adopted son *must be* my child.'"

"And is that the complete and correct statement that Mrs. Greer made to you at that time?" the lawyer asked.

What were the exact words? What difference did it make anyway? the woman pondered.

"I am trying to collect my thoughts. That wasn't yesterday," she said.

The best way it could be left, then, Wells decided, was by taking a lawyer's refuge in a witness's "best recollection." So he asked, "Is that the best recollection you have, Annie?"

"That is the best I have, yes," the woman conceded.

Pursuing his point—that Mrs. Greer did not identify her son with Harold Segur other than by supposing that Dr. Segur's adopted son was her son—Wells continued, "Did she ever furnish any name to you as the name of this child?"

"She used to say 'Little Bill.' That is what she said. She always called him either 'Little Bill' or 'The Boy.'"

"Now, Annie," the lawyer continued, "you told us that Mrs. Greer said the child had been born in a boarding house in Boston. Did she tell you who was present at the time the child was born?"

"Dr. Segur was present."

"Did she say anyone else was present?"

"The woman that owned the boarding house."

"Did Mrs. Greer mention any other persons who might have been present?"

"No, there wasn't."

"What did she do with the child, as she told it to you, Annie?"

"She left the child on the bed of the woman that owned the boarding house and asked the woman if she would look after the child until she returned."

"Did she tell you if she ever returned?"

"She told me she did not and never saw the child again."

"Did she tell you how old she was at the time she had this child?"

"In her early teens—that is what she said."

Wells paused. He had drawn from the witness all he could expect. Just what Mrs. Greer had told her about the adoption was rendered doubtful. He was prepared to argue on the basis of her testimony that all Mrs. Greer had said about the adoption was merely a deduction or rationalization from what she had read in the paper in 1939. It was notable to his mind that although Mrs. Greer had told the witness of the birth and abandonment of the child long before, she had said nothing about an adoption until she read of the doctor's death and of his leaving an adopted child.

One other thing came to his mind, a strange story this faithful servant had told him of another conversation with Mrs. Greer. It didn't help his case except perhaps in one particular. Nevertheless, he felt impelled to bring it out.

"Did Mrs. Greer at one time have a leather wallet?" he asked.

"Yes."

"Can you recall the time of a conversation with her about the wallet?"

"Yes. It was last July," she recalled. "I can't give you the exact day, but about two weeks before she passed away. She was in bed. She told me where to go and I would find a box, and I brought the box and, in the box, as I put it on her bed, she looked through until she found this wallet. When she found it she took it out. I carried the box back, put it in its usual place. When I came back to her bed she said to me that 'I have kept this wallet all these years, hoping that my son would come. Now that Mr. Greer has gone, when I see him I am going to give him this wallet,' she said, 'with a nice check in it.'"

"Did she mention anything about a trip that she was going to take?"

"She said in September she hoped that she would be well enough to go to Boston to look, she said, 'for my boy.'"

"Did she say what she would do when she found him?"

"Well, she had told me all along what she wanted to do. She wanted to see him and let him see her; that she was his mother and she had never done anything for him, and she wanted to do something for him."

Wells sat down, reflecting on the sad note of a mother's last generous thoughts of a neglected child. Whatever sympathy was engendered for either was beside the point, however. The point, to him, was that Mrs. Greer to the end was thinking of her son as being in Boston, not Worcester.

Cox had listened attentively to the examination and cross-examination of the witness, wondering whether to put any questions himself. It was the last line of testimony that decided him. That seemed promising and worth pursuing.

With directness he asked, "Did Mrs. Greer ever tell you where her boy lived?"

"Well, she didn't know where he lived. Only left him in the boarding house. She didn't know."

"Subsequent to 1939, did Mrs. Greer ever tell you that she was trying to communicate with her boy?"

"No. I knew she was not, for the reason that she had the fear of Mr. Greer knowing, and she didn't try."

"After Mr. Greer's death, what did Mrs. Greer tell you about the boy?"

"She wanted to see him. She wanted to go and look for him, and that was the one thought she had."

But she evidently didn't know where to find him, Cox thought, and that belied her professed belief that he was the adopted son of Dr. Segur.

Now, perhaps the witness could contribute something on the matter of age. Questions of age were going to haunt this case, Cox knew—Mrs. Greer's age, her son's age, even the doctor's age when the child was born.

"After Mr. Greer's death did Mrs. Greer indicate to you how old her boy was or would be at that time?" he asked.

The answer indicated something about Mrs. Greer, but nothing about age: "Mrs. Greer never talked much of age—never."

"Did she talk about the boy's age?"

"She didn't talk about her boy's age, nor did she talk about her own age."

"Did she indicate to you how old the doctor, who was the father of the child, was at the time of the birth of the child?"

"He was very young. That is the way she put it to me. She said, 'We both were very young.'"

"But she indicated that the father of the child was a doctor?"

"He hadn't finished school at that time, she said, but he was studying to be a doctor, so, of course, she always referred to him as 'doctor.' That is the way she addressed him to me."

Cox next had the witness repeat what she had told Wells respecting the birth of the child, that only Dr. Segur and the lady who operated the boarding house were present—no other doctor was there. This was contradictory, he knew, to what Mrs. Greer had told Armbruster at another and later time. That would come out too, and he wanted to point up the contradiction for the purpose of arguing that Mrs. Greer was not a reliable reporter of events respecting the child.

If one really knew who was present at the birth of the child, Cox thought, and that person was living and could be found, the correct answer to several crucial questions could be found. But the birth seemed shrouded in mystery, or fancy, as was Mrs. Greer. And who was Mrs. Greer? One might have to know that before one could find out who or where her child was. But all information vital to the search for the son seemed to be buried in a past before the time that anyone living knew or could place Mrs. Greer.

No birth certificate or papers of any kind had been discovered which shed any light on her identity prior to her marriage other than her application for a marriage licence. In that paper, made out in November 1908, she stated that she was twenty-seven and had been born in Manchester, England, the daughter of a James Seymour and Charlotte Barnes. No pains had been spared to verify this information. Diligent inquiry had been made not only in Manchester but in London, where all vital statistics of England were kept, but no record of a birth of a Mabel Seymour to a James Seymour and Charlotte Barnes had been uncovered.

The disclosures following her death had given rise to many rumours concerning her past life. But none of them, when tracked down led anywhere. None of her known friends could contribute anything on the subject of her ancestry or early life. Here before the court now was her oldest retainer, servant, companion and confidante. What did she know of Mrs. Greer prior to her becoming Mrs. Greer?

"Did Mrs. Greer tell you what she was doing in Boston at the time of the birth of this child?" Cox inquired.

"No."

"Did she tell you whether she was working at anything?"

"No."

"Did she ever tell you whether or not she had worked at all before her marriage to Mr. Greer?"

"No."

"Did she say anything about her life before she met Mr. Greer?"

"No."

"Did she tell you what her maiden name was before she married Mr. Greer?"

"Well, she went by—she was called Mabel Seymour."

"Was that the only other name that you knew?"

"That is the only one I knew."

Cox was finished. Friedman was prompted by the cross-examination to put only one further question before releasing the witness—the crucial question of age. Friedman knew that on the basis of the record of Mrs. Greer's age, as made in her application for a marriage licence, the opposition was going to argue that she was much too young to be the mother of Harold Segur. But he did not accept that record and was going to challenge it at every opportunity.

Cox had skirted with Mrs. Jackson the question of Mrs. Greer's age and had drawn a blank on the question of what Mrs. Greer had told her of the boy's age. But both Wells and Cox had been too canny to open up the question of Mrs. Greer's age with the witness. They had solid documentary evidence, in the form of the application for a marriage licence, supporting their position as to her age, and unless and until it was shaken they would not invite what they considered the less probative and more arguable opinion of witnesses. Friedman, on the other hand, was obliged to resort to such evidence and to place reliance on it. He could get something from Mrs. Jackson as to her observations of Mrs. Greer's apparent age.

"Mrs. Jackson," he asked, "what in your opinion was the age of Mrs. Greer at the time of her death?"

According to the age stated in her application for a marriage licence, Mrs. Greer would have been sixty-five at the time of her death.

"Well," the witness replied, "I would say that in my opinion she would be somewhere between seventy-three and seventy-four."

Wells, for his last chance to add to the servant's testimony, thought it worth while only to check the opinion she had just expressed as to Mrs. Greer's age at the time of her death with the opinion she might have of Mrs. Greer's age as she appeared in her wedding photograph taken in 1908, when she was supposed to be twenty-seven.

"I show you this photograph of Mrs. Greer," he said, "and ask you to examine it carefully and tell me how old Mrs. Greer appears to be in that photograph."

"I would say that she was in her early thirties."

"Can you make it more definite than that?"

"Well, it is kind of hard to just say, but I would say between thirty-one and thirty-two—something like that."

The lawyers were finished with the first witness. The judge made another gesture. It was one of dismissal. Annie Jackson stepped down and out into a world of memories.

6

Dr. and Mrs. Tierney—Keepers
of a Confidence

* * * * *

"YOUR next witness, please, Mr. Friedman." The crisp tone of the judge indicated that there was to be no pause in the proceeding.

"Dr. Tierney," the lawyer called, "Dr. William J. Tierney."

The professional poise and ease with which the doctor was accustomed to lean back in his office chair and listen encouragingly to the complaints of patients was absent as he took the witness stand and sat forward in the chair, obviously intent on dispatching his departure.

"Dr. Tierney, how long did you know Mrs. Greer?"

That single question was all that was required to bring forth what was on the doctor's mind, a professional privilege which he hoped would spare his time here. Not a moment was to be lost in asserting it.

"Now, your Honour," he began, "I think it is my duty to acquaint the court with the fact that any testimony I am expected to give here is confidential, as between physician and his patient."

The judge was cuttingly short. "There is no such rule of law, Doctor. There may be some aspects of a doctor's relation with his patient which are confidential, but not his total contacts with her. Answer the question. How long did you know her?"

The doctor sat back and answered, "I have known Mrs. Greer since 1908. I was staying at a summer hotel at Lake Mohegan. Mrs. Greer was staying there also and was taken sick and she wished to have me prescribe for her."

Friedman resumed the questioning without further demur from the witness.

Mrs. Greer was known as Mabel Seymour when the doctor first met her. He continued a professional relationship with her after her marriage, and his wife and Mrs. Greer became very friendly and visited back and forth. A year or two after her marriage, Mrs. Greer told him that she had had a child and passed its care over to somebody else and had not seen the child since. The father was described as a prominent doctor in Boston, but he was not named.

The witness had not been told how old Mrs. Greer was when she gave birth to the child. He had never asked Mrs. Greer how old she was during the time he knew her because professionally, he emphasized, he didn't have to. He attended her wedding and from his recollection of her at that time and from her picture he would say that she was about thirty in 1908.

Mrs. Greer never made mention of her son again until many years later. Then she said that someone claiming to be her son had spoken to her chauffeur at the Piping Rock Club and she asked the doctor what he thought of it.

"Well, to be candid with you," the doctor replied, "I don't think much about it, because I think if the man whom you mention was your son, he would have come to you and not to your chauffeur." He added, "I should have him produce pretty good evidence, excellent evidence, as to who he is before you have anything to do with him. If he can't do that and doesn't come to you directly, then I wouldn't consider him at all."

"Did Mrs. Greer ever mention this incident at any later date to you?" Wells inquired in his turn.

"Yes," the doctor recalled, "she mentioned it shortly before she died. She said that she was going to make a will the next day and that she had remembered what I had said to her, and that she had never heard about him since. That was all. She had never heard about him since, and I knew who she meant by that."

Relieved when the lawyer sat down and no one else arose to continue the questioning, the witness felt rewarded when the judge cut in this time to say, "You are excused, Doctor."

Mrs. Tierney was not so reluctant as her husband. She felt that the confidences she had received from her old friend over the years might shed some light on the mystery of the day and might aid in identifying the son of whom Mrs. Greer had spoken so often. She liked the idea of his coming into his own and of herself being an instrument of justice. She also sat forward in the witness chair, but more with anticipation than annoyance.

Friedman started. "Mrs. Tierney, you are the wife of Dr. Tierney. Did you know Mrs. Greer during her lifetime?"

"I knew her for thirty-eight years," the witness proclaimed.

"How frequently did you visit Mrs. Greer socially?"

"Why, Mrs. Greer and I were together all the time. We went down to the stores and travelled around together. We were very friendly."

"Did Mrs. Greer ever tell you that she had given birth to a son?"

"Yes." The lady settled in. "Mrs. Greer called me up about fifteen years ago, and I knew she had been crying, and I asked her what was wrong. She said, 'I want to tell you something and if I come up in the car, will you come over to the park?' So Frank—he was her chauffeur—brought us over to the park."

"What did Mrs. Greer tell you at that time?"

"Mrs. Greer told me, 'I have a surprise for you. I am terribly mixed up.' Then she said, 'I had a son born before I married Mr. Greer,' and I said, 'Were you married before?' I thought maybe she had been. She said, 'No,' and she said, 'After the baby was born'—and she started right on the story—she said, 'After the baby was born I went down and bought a christening robe for the baby. I insisted upon having the child baptized. I saw to that.' Then she said the doctor wanted to keep the baby, but she didn't want to give it up, so she walked around Boston crying. She didn't have any money, and she walked around. Then she finally saw some church open, and she sat down there to think things over and she found there was no way she could keep the child, so she had the child's picture taken, and then she brought the child back and gave it up to some woman there."

"How many times did Mrs. Greer speak to you about her son?" Friedman continued.

"That was the only time, before Mr. Greer died—she was always afraid Mr. Greer would hear about it. She spoke about the child a great deal after Mr. Greer died."

"How many times altogether?"

"I can't tell you. After Mr. Greer died she spoke about him all the time. She was very anxious for him to come and see her."

Friedman stopped and thought for a moment. He decided to try to learn something of Mrs. Greer's background from this old and trusted friend, but received in return only the usual answers.

"Did Mrs. Greer ever tell you where she was born?" he inquired.

"No."

"Did she ever tell you how old she was?"

"No."

"Did she ever tell you what she had done for her livelihood prior to her marriage to Mr. Greer?"

"No."

It was Wells's turn. He asked, "How did Mrs. Greer identify the father of the child? Did she call him by name?"

"No, I never heard his name. She always said, 'the doctor from Boston.' She called him a cousin."

"Did she tell you that she had ever heard from the doctor after the child's birth?"

"She said that she had never heard from him."

"Did she ever mention anything about an adoption of the child?"

"No."

Wells was interested in whether the chauffeur could have overheard the original conversation between Mrs. Greer and Mrs. Tierney about the birth of the child and inquired whether he had been within earshot or in the immediate vicinity at that time.

"No," the witness replied. "She told Frank to go and have a smoke—have a walk and smoke."

"Did Mrs. Greer ever tell you that she had told the story to Frank?"

"I don't know that she had before that time. Afterwards she told me that she had told Frank."

"When did she tell you that?"

"It was about four years ago. Mrs. Greer came from the Piping Rock Club, and she was quite worked up. She had asked Frank to bring her up to see me. It seems that she and Mr. Greer were staying at the Piping Rock Club, that he was in town that day and she was going for a ride, that she went out as happy as could be. She got in the car and Frank handed her a card and said, 'A gentleman gave me this card to give you,' and Mrs. Greer took the card and saw the name on it and almost fainted. She said, 'Frank, take me back. We will pack up and leave the hotel right away.' And they did, and when they were coming home Mrs. Greer almost collapsed and she said, 'Frank, stop—I can't go any further,' and then Frank said, 'What's the matter with you?' and she told Frank the story."

"Did she tell you what name appeared on the card?"

"No, she didn't."

"Continue please."

"So then she—of course, she was in a terrible way; she was crying and going on that way, and I told her that she would have to stop thinking about it because she had to go home and face Mr. Greer, and to pick herself up—and so she took my advice and went home, and then she telephoned me that night. She said, 'I was fine all through dinner.'"

Cox, who had seemed absorbed in rolling a pencil between the palms of his hands all during the examination of the witness, looked up as Wells sat down and, taking a moment to resolve a train of thought, he asked, "There was no conversation about the photograph which Mrs. Greer told you she had taken of her child, other than what you have told us?"

"No, except about four weeks before she died she said, 'You know I have the baby's picture.' I said, 'Have you? Where is it?' and she said, 'It is in the drawer with my papers.'"

Cox did not conceal his surprise at this disclosure. He presumed the witness was telling the truth. There was no reason for her to falsify. But he rather guessed that Mrs. Greer was fancifying at the time. Her papers had been carefully combed after her death and there had been no baby picture among them.

"Did you ever see the photograph?" he asked.

"No, I never did," the witness acknowledged.

The expectations of a lawyer from a witness are not always fulfilled, no matter how carefully the witness has been interviewed or prepared. Even direct examination in court of one's own witness is accompanied by a certain wonder and worry as to what he will say. And a lawyer is always on pins and needles during cross-examination by an adversary. Will he cross the witness up, impair the favourable testimony given, or bring out something positively favourable to the other side? Sometimes it works the other way, and a witness is better on cross-examination than on direct. He may bring out something surprisingly good. On such an occasion a lawyer sits by with delight as his adversary "shakes the Christmas tree".

Some of these thoughts ran through Friedman's mind as he listened to the cross-examination of Mrs. Tierney. He was not disturbed by it, although there were no gifts in it either. He could wish that she would answer differently Wells's question of whether Mrs. Greer had ever said anything about an adoption of the child. He had not touched on that subject on direct and it would have been doubly good if the witness had answered affirmatively on cross. Might she still possibly do so if the question were put in coaxing form? Nothing ventured, nothing gained, so Friedman ventured on a redirect examination.

"Didn't Mrs. Greer ever tell you that the doctor had adopted the boy?" The insinuation in the inflection was that Mrs. Greer must have told Mrs. Tierney of the adoption.

"No" was the immediate response, and then in a twinkling of remembrance: "Oh, yes, she did. He was to adopt the boy."

"When did she tell you that?"

"Well, I think she heard that after the doctor died. Could she have heard that after the doctor died?"

"I am asking *you* when she told it to you," the lawyer prompted.

"Now, it might have been after the doctor died." Mrs. Tierney was trying to remember. "Yes, she told me that the boy had been adopted and that he had been sent to a very good school, and the doctor spent quite a little money on him, was very liberal, was very generous with him."

Not so good as it might have been, but still worth while, Friedman thought, and enough to nettle Wells, who now fairly jumped at the witness.

"Mrs. Tierney, a little earlier, if you recall, I asked you if Mrs. Greer had ever said anything about the child being adopted and you said, 'No.' Do you remember?"

"I will correct that," the witness said apologetically but firmly. "Mrs. Greer did tell me, yes, the child was adopted and the doctor was very, very good to him."

"When did she tell you that, Mrs. Tierney?"

"After the doctor died. I don't think Mrs. Greer knew it before."

"How did the subject of adoption come up?"

"She was talking about the doctor's death, and she told me there was a great account in the paper about it. I think that is the day she must have told me he adopted the boy."

"Did she tell you that she heard about the adoption after she had read the newspaper?"

"She told me afterwards, yes. She only told me that she heard the boy was adopted. The doctor adopted him and sent him to

[43]

very good schools, spent quite a little money on him, very well educated. He is a graduate of what college? Now, wait, Dartmouth, isn't it?"

"Where did you hear, or where did you see the name Dartmouth, Mrs. Tierney?" Wells was exacting.

Mrs. Tierney melted. "Well, you know Mrs. Greer used to wander off and tell me some yarns, and that might have been one of the yarns, because I think it came from Mrs. Greer."

"And that was about the time she mentioned the account of the doctor's death in the newspaper?"

"Yes, it was all about the same week, you know."

Wells nodded his head in emphasis and sat down. The witness waited. The judge looked at the clock with its hands at four. "We will adjourn for the day," he said.

All rose, and the judge departed, leaving the lawyers standing. As they gathered their papers together, Cox thought out loud, "I wonder if Mrs. Greer really did have a baby picture of the child, and if so what became of it?"

To his surprise, Friedman answered, "I can tell you."

Cox looked at him and said mockingly, "Can you really?" awaiting the suggestion that someone connected with the bank and interested in sustaining the will had come upon the photograph and done away with it.

"Well, I can't really, but I can make a shrewd guess," Friedman replied. He waited a second to enjoy the other's curiosity, then went on. "I think Annie Jackson destroyed it in a misguided moment, not knowing that the existence of a child would ever come out and thinking that she was protecting Mrs. Greer's memory in some way by not letting the baby picture be found.

"Understand," he added, "I am only guessing. I haven't asked and wouldn't embarrass that good woman by asking. But you can bet that's what happened, although there is no way of collecting the bet."

"Uhm," muttered Cox, as he stuffed the rest of his papers into his briefcase.

7

A Letter

* * * * *

WITNESSES can come in strange ways. Jennie Sheppard came by letter. Out of the blue, manna from heaven, answer to a prayer. Lester Friedman had not actually prayed. He was a religious man and would not invoke the Deity for aid in a lawsuit. But he had cogitated long on how he might find a witness who knew Mrs. Greer back in the days before she was Mrs. Greer, and who knew—or at least had been told by Mrs. Greer close to the time of the event—that her child had been adopted by Dr. Segur.

Friedman was fully conscious of the weakness in his case. The chain of proof consisted of several links, but it hinged on the link of Dr. Segur's adopting Mabel Seymour's child. Wells and Cox would hammer away at that link. All that Friedman had to forge it with—until he received the letter—were statements made by Mrs. Greer long after the event, when it was questionable whether she spoke from actual knowledge or mere supposition from what she read in the newspaper after Dr. Segur's death.

So Friedman had said to himself, If only there were someone somewhere who knew the facts and could be found and brought forward, the case could be wrapped up in ribbons. The someone would be an old lady by now, someone who had lived around Boston in the 1880s or 90s. But there wasn't a thing to go on, and one couldn't wander around Boston asking every old lady if she had known a person called Mabel Seymour fifty years ago.

Then one morning, when Friedman sat down at his desk to open the usual mail and start the usual day, there was an unusual letter awaiting him. A plain envelope, addressed in a not too firm hand, and rather bulky in content. There were several pages. It started, "You don't know me, but . . ." But! Were the eyes to be believed? Could it be true—all for the asking, even without the asking?

The letter was signed "Jennie Sheppard," and the address was 243 East 124th Street, New York City.

This was not the first letter Friedman had received from unknown correspondents offering to be helpful and volunteering information about the past life of Mrs. Greer. The newspapers had been full of the case, with photographs of Mrs. Greer and the story of her known life. The mystery of her unknown life was posed, and this was public invitation to anyone who knew anything of her past to come forward and offer assistance. Friedman had a file of such letters. They were interesting but not helpful. They told quite some stories, but a responsible lawyer would not present the writers as witnesses without some verification of their information, and the verification was not forthcoming. Anyway, most of what was written told only about Mrs. Greer without shedding any light on the identity of her child.

Jennie Sheppard, however, was the exception. What she

wrote was of genuine interest and the utmost significance—if it was true.

The next day Jennie Sheppard sat across the desk from Friedman, a woman well into her seventies, with strong features, accentuated cheekbones in a long but full face, and snapping dark-brown eyes under straggling grey-white hair. The shabbiness of dress was not in keeping with her positive personality. It did not indicate poverty so much as lack of care about her appearance. She was not interested in money; she made that clear at the outset. She wanted nothing except to tell what she knew. That she told volubly and with zeal.

Friedman listened, questioned. Doubts could not be resolved. There was no way to check the story beyond the fact that the woman had lived in Worcester a half century before. She was willing to be tested by all manner of questions at every point of her story. But the questioning could neither prove nor disprove the essential facts. Jennie Sheppard would have to be offered as a witness on her own. Friedman hoped that she would carry conviction.

8

Jennie Sheppard—From
the Long Ago

* * * * *

"MRS. SHEPPARD, I show you this photograph and ask you whether you know this lady."

Glancing at the photograph of Mrs. Greer in her wedding dress, the witness snapped out, "Mabel Seymour."

"When did you first meet Mabel Seymour?"

"My husband was coming in from Boston——"

Already Friedman was beginning to fear garrulousness. He cut in, "When was that? How long ago?"

"It was Christmas Eve."

"How long ago?"

"Well, about fifty-two years ago."

"Where were you living at that time?"

"One ninety-two Chandler Street, Worcester, Massachusetts."

"Did she come alone or did she come with somebody?"

"My husband brought her."

"What were the circumstances?"

"He said she was poor and she was looking for a place to live, and he asked if I could make room for her, so I says, 'Bring her in.'"

The Sheppard family at that time, she said, consisted of her husband, herself and their two-year-old son, Mannie. Mabel Seymour stayed with them until March.

"During the time that she was with you at your home, did Mabel Seymour do any work?" Friedman asked.

"Yes. She helped me with the housework. She was an adorable, well-behaved girl."

"Besides doing work at your home, did she do any other work?"

"Yes. I took her on the road with me after New Year's. We went to Hill's Envelope Shop and we got linen stationery, and we sold it up through the farm roads."

"Did Mabel Seymour ever tell you anything about her personal life?"

"Yes. She said she would like to confide in me, and I told her to go ahead. She told me that she had been going with a young man by the name of Willard Segur who was studying medicine in Boston, and he had promised to marry her, and that she had become the mother of his little boy."

"Did she tell you what had become of the boy?"

"She said that she put him in a safe place, something like a boarding house, and that Willard Segur had an understanding with her to keep, you know, scandal off of both sides; that in time he would take the boy out, like adopt him, and would raise him in his home."

All eyes were riveted on the witness, and judge and opposing counsel were listening with rapt attention and full consciousness of the import of the testimony as Friedman moved on with the examination.

"Did she tell you how old the boy was?"

"No. She told me that the boy was older than my boy."

"Do you remember when your boy Mannie was born?"

"Well, November will be fifty-five years."

"That means he was born in 1892. Is that correct?"

"Yes."

"Then when Mabel Seymour was in your home in Worcester, when Mannie was a little over two years old, that was in 1894?"

"Yes."

"Do you know how old Mabel Seymour was at that time?"

"Well, she looked to me like twenty-four or twenty-five. I didn't question her, because I thought she may not like it."

"Now, you say that Mabel Seymour left your home in the early part of March of 1895. Did she tell you where she was going?"

"Yes. She said she was going to New York City to try and get a position."

"Did she tell you what kind of position she was going to try to get?"

"Well, like at a hotel, a chambermaid—something like that."

"Did you see Mabel Seymour again after that?" The question was a signal of something even more portentous to come.

Only once, the old lady replied, fifteen years later. It was in Worcester when Mannie was seventeen years old. She placed the time by his having chicken pox at the time. It was not at the same house which Mabel Seymour had visited before. She came unannounced, out of the blue, saying that she had located Mrs. Sheppard through a friend in New York.

"Did you ask her about her life?" Friedman inquired.

"Yes. I asked her how she was getting along. She told me she was very happy. She married a rich man and she was very happy, but she felt depressed for the boy."

"Did you ask her anything about the boy?"

"Yes. I asked—I says, 'Mabel, do you ever see your little son?'

She said, 'No.' She says Willard had made his promise good. He took him in his home and he is raising him. He adopted him right out."

There it was—a contemporary confirmation of the adoption, indubitably pointing to Harold Segur as the son of Mrs. Greer and, if it was to be believed, blasting the notion advanced by Wells and Cox that Mrs. Greer's later statements that her son was adopted by Dr. Segur were mere inference drawn from his obituary.

Friedman allowed it full effect before putting his next and last questions.

"Did you ask Mabel Seymour the name of the man whom she married?"

"She wouldn't tell me. She never wanted him to know anything."

"How long did she visit with you that second time?"

"She just came for the day, came through from New York, and then she took me into Richard Healy's. Richard Healy kept a department store, and she bought me a dress. Then she left, going towards evening, but before she left she shook hands with me, bid me good-bye, and gave me ten ten-dollar gold pieces—one hundred dollars altogether. She says, 'You were good to me. You gave me shelter. You threw your home open to me. Go home now, make a good supper.'"

"After Mabel Seymour left you that second time, you never saw her again?"

"No. I never seen her again."

Slowly and quietly Friedman retired to his seat, leaving a full courtroom under the spell of the old woman's homely account of her last meeting with Mabel Seymour.

9

Jennie Sheppard—Truth or Fancy?

* * * * *

"MAY we have a short recess before cross-examination, your Honour?" Wells asked the court. "I should like to confer with Mr. Cox."

The request was not unexpected. "Certainly," the judge replied. His thoughts were reflected by Cox's query of Wells as the two lawyers went into a huddle in the corridor.

"Is she telling the truth or is that story made out of whole cloth?"

"There isn't a word of truth in it, in my opinion," Wells replied. "She is a fanciful old woman and dreamed up that tale."

"But can you prove it?" Cox asked. "She is an eccentric, but she looks honest, and there are no two ways about it—either she is telling the truth, in which case we might as well concede that Segur is the child, or she's a complete fake. It will take some doing to blow her up."

"There's only one way," Wells answered. "A painstaking cross-examination. Questioning on some minute details. Her story is pat enough in outline, but can she fill in the details?

E

You just can't make them up as you go along. We must not spare her. Give her a lot of rope, you know. That is the way."

"Right," Cox agreed.

The lawyers then returned to their task.

"How many years ago was that, Mrs. Sheppard, that you first met Miss Seymour?" Wells began.

"Fifty-two years ago."

"What makes you so certain in your mind it was fifty-two years ago?"

"On account of my little boy's age."

"When was he born?"

"He was born November third."

"What year?"

"I never kept any remembrance of any years," the witness asserted with disdain.

"You can't remember the year?"

"No, I never kept it."

"You can remember how many years ago it was that you met Mrs. Greer?"

"He was two years old when she came in," the woman reiterated, referring back to her son's age at the time, "and that would make it fifty-two. He is fifty-five now—he will be, in November."

"But you can't remember the date when your son was born?"

"Oh, yes—the third of November."

"I am talking about the year, Mrs. Sheppard."

"I never—I didn't have the patience to write it down, but my boy knows in Worcester." That settled it in her estimation.

Wells shifted. "Where were you born?" he asked.

"New York City."

"Give me the year, the date and the month." He was going to become exacting.

"I think I was born in 1870."

"Did you get any birth certificate to prove your birth?"

"No."

"Were you baptized?"

"Well, we are Jewish, you know. Jewish people don't get baptized."

"Do you recall what year you were married?"

"Yes. The first of April."

Wells raised his voice. "What year?"

"My mother had died and a week after that I got married," the witness rejoined. "She's dead fifty-seven years now."

"I am asking you to tell me what year." Wells spoke with accentuated distinctness to indicate insistence on a responsive answer.

"I told you," the old lady replied, insisting on her own way of calculating years by referring backward to some significant event in her life. "I never marked it down, but I do know I was married that long. All I know, it was April Fool that Sunday."

Wells strategically retreated to other ground. He inquired as to Mrs. Sheppard's family and the living arrangements in her Worcester home when Mabel Seymour lodged there.

Her husband was dead, the witness said. She had two living children, neither of whom would have known anything about Mabel Seymour. The house on Chandler Street, Worcester, where Mabel Seymour appeared that Christmas Eve fifty-two years ago, was a rooming house, in which the Sheppards rented three rooms and a little spare room on the ground floor. Mabel Seymour was given the little spare room off the side of the

[55]

kitchen, just large enough to hold a couch. A month ago Mrs. Sheppard had visited her son in Massachusetts and they had gone together to see the house. She wanted to see if it was still standing.

This trip to see the house interested Wells and prompted an inquiry as to when and how Mrs. Sheppard came into the case.

"You had known about this case in March, then, when you went up to look the house over?" he asked.

"Oh, I heard about the case," the witness acknowledged.

"How long have you known about the case?"

"Oh, I have been reading the papers right along. You know, I am an American-born woman. And then, when I seen the names Seymour and Segur, it all came back to me. So I sat down and I wrote a letter to Mr. Friedman."

"How did you get his name?"

"In the paper. He didn't know me. I didn't know him either."

"Did you write the letter before March?"

"I wrote a letter—I can't remember when I wrote it—and then, when he got the letter, he thought it over."

"How do you know he thought it over?"

"He wanted to know if I am telling the truth."

Friedman, who was listening tensely to the cross-examination of his witness, relaxed for a second and mentally clapped his hands at this spontaneous demonstration of good faith.

"What did you say in that letter, do you remember?" Wells continued.

Her hands went up. "Oh, my God! Can I remember everything I said?"

"Tell us in general what you said?" Wells pursued, unruffled.

"I sent him a very nice, interesting letter."

"Was it a long letter?" the lawyer asked teasingly.

"Yes, a nice, long letter," the witness admitted readily, "and when he seen that letter and read it he says—well, then he sent somebody after me."

"Was it before or after you wrote that letter that you went to Worcester, Massachusetts?"

"Oh, I wrote it long before that, before I went to Worcester."

"What was the purpose of your going to Worcester?" Wells wanted to know. "Just to visit, or did you want to examine something about this case?"

"No, sir, I didn't go to examine no case," was the firm response. "All I went for was to see my boy, because he was ill."

"Had anybody spoken to you about ascertaining whether the house in Worcester that you have testified to was still standing?"

"Nobody spoke to me about that," the witness said emphatically. "I myself took my boy with me and I says, 'Come, Mannie, I want to see if that house is still there.'"

"Is it still standing?"

"It is standing, but it was fixed over."

"What does it look like today? Will you describe it?"

"Oh, some old-fashioned shack."

"How many floors?"

"There is like two now. There is like a little store down the side—I didn't take notice—and there is a coloured family, and he said he lived there thirty-five years."

Wells was feeling his way. He had to admit that he had not yet found a soft spot in the testimony to drive through. The old woman with whom he had been jousting for some time now had stood her ground, altogether composed, and in her own way had been precise and had parried his thrusts. He would continue, however, to try to trap her on specific details.

"You say that Mabel Seymour arrived at your house fifty-two

years ago Christmas Eve. What time of the day was it that she arrived there?"

"It was half past seven at night" was the surprisingly precise reply.

"How do you know it was seven-thirty?"

"Because I remember the clock when my husband walked in."

"Did you look at the clock when he walked in?"

"I looked at the clock because I expected him in and he wasn't in yet. That is how I happened to know the time."

"Weren't you a little surprised to see a woman walking in with your husband?" Wells looked surprised.

"Why was I surprised? I trusted him," she shot back.

"Had you or your husband known this woman before she arrived there that night?"

"Never in his life. He was coming off a Boston train and she was a poor girl, and she said that she would like to get a room in some rooming house where she could live."

"Did you ask your husband how he came to meet this woman?"

"Well, they got in conversation, you know, talking on the train. He pitied her because she looked pitiful."

"Did you ask her if she had any money?"

"I didn't ask her, but she told me herself she had twenty-five dollars."

What explanation had Mabel Seymour given for landing in Worcester? What had she been doing in Boston? What of her family? the lawyer asked. Nothing had been said on those subjects, the witness replied, except that Mabel had been doing some kind of little work for which she got paid ten cents an hour. She had no people.

[58]

"How tall did she appear to you to be at the time?" Wells asked.

"A little taller than me" was the relative answer.

"How tall are you?"

Standing up, the witness replied, "You can see. She was a little bit taller."

"What was her weight, as you could best gauge it at that time?"

"Her weight? I never sized her up, you know."

"Was she a stout woman?"

"She was thin. She wasn't fat. She wasn't stout. Not in them days."

"What colour hair did she have?"

"Her hair was like a chestnut brown, dark."

"What was the manner of her speech? Did she talk like you, rapidly?"

"She spoke very nice. I never noticed whether she spoke rapid or not."

"Did she speak in a slow manner when you first saw her?"

"I don't know. She was nice-spoken. That is all I know."

"When she spoke to you, what did you observe, if anything, with regard to the tone or accent of her voice? Was it a Boston accent, do you remember?"

"There was a little accent there. I don't know. It could be like down East, you know, or it could be like a little English accent, you know. A little bit. Not much, though."

"You can't characterize it as to what it was?" the lawyer pursued.

"No. I just know she was nice-spoken—that is all." And that was all the witness would say.

"You spoke to her some years after that, didn't you?"

"Yes, but I didn't take notice of that. Remember, I am an old woman. You think I can have that all on my mind?"

Wells did not propose to give any quarter or permit her to take refuge in her old age. He pressed on. "Had her voice changed any since the time you first spoke to her?"

"No. She was nice-spoken. She talked more like the New Yorkers talk. She got that way."

"How much did this woman pay you for this little kitchen bedroom?"

"I wouldn't take a penny from her. I threw my home open to her. I didn't want no money. She said she would never forget me."

The lawyer eyed his quarry. "Did you ever throw your home open to anybody else before or after that incident?" he asked. "Just take them off the street?"

"Just that poor girl. She was a nice, well-behaved girl."

"You didn't know it at the time?" he suggested.

"When she came to my home she was adorable. I liked her. She was a nice girl," the witness repeated firmly.

Wells was curious as to how Mrs. Greer had found Mrs. Sheppard the second time fifteen years later, when Mrs. Sheppard had moved in the meantime, and he bore down in questioning on that point.

The witness said that she had a friend in New York City by the name of Mae Schoell who had met Mrs. Greer in Scroub's Oyster & Chop House on 125th Street, and Mrs. Greer learned in that way of Mrs. Sheppard's address.

A strange place for Mrs. Greer to be, Wells reflected. It was home territory for Mrs. Sheppard, but hardly for Mrs. Greer.

"Will you tell us how she happened to find out your address from this party on 125th Street?" he asked.

"Yes, I will," the witness answered obligingly. "Mae invited her up to her house. Mae didn't know that she knew me, and she seen my picture on the wall and she says to Mae, 'How do you come to have that picture? That is Sheppie.' Mae says, 'You know Sheppie?' Mabel says, 'She threw her home open to me, gave me shelter when I needed it very bad. Where does Sheppie live now?' Then, all of a sudden, from an open sky, she flew in on me and spent a few hours and then went back the same day."

"Was this woman who had your picture a close personal friend of yours, this Mae?"

"Yes."

"Is she still living?" the lawyer asked in a tone of mock expectancy.

"No. She died in April."

Wells nodded his head meaningfully.

He decided to revert to the day Mabel Seymour first arrived in Worcester, and he asked for more details. Did she have a bag?

"She might have had a little satchel or something. I could hardly remember that."

Was she wearing an overcoat?

"A little black Newmarket. It was winter, cold."

Mrs. Sheppard gave her neither money nor clothes, nor did she take any money from her. But Mabel earned a little money on the road, selling stationery, and had a hundred dollars when she left.

Wells jumped forward again to the second visit. What became of the ten-dollar gold pieces? She had kept them for twenty years and then had turned them in at the Harlem Savings Bank, Mrs. Sheppard explained.

[61]

"Where did you keep those ten-dollar gold pieces until you finally disposed of them?" he asked.

"Where did I keep them? Don't you know where a woman keeps money?" she asked in reply, seizing a chance to chide the lawyer.

"No. I am asking you the question, madam," Wells reminded her stiffly.

"I kept them in my hose."

Shifting to the witness's recent trip to Worcester, when she looked up the old house where Mabel Seymour had stayed, the lawyer asked, "Have you been repaid your expense of going to Worcester by anybody?"

"Nobody ever paid money for me," she responded proudly.

"Have you asked anybody to pay for your trip to Worcester?"

"Oh, please. I never had no home relief or old pension, so I surely didn't need anyone to pay."

Was there any connection then between Harold Segur and her visit to Worcester, or was she altogether on her own? Wells inquired. The woman replied that she had never spoken to Harold Segur and had never seen him until she saw him in the courtroom. She had made no effort to get in touch with him when she was in Worcester in March.

"You were interested in locating this house, but you were not interested in contacting Mr. Segur. Is that correct?"

The rhetorical question provoked the old lady's sense of self-justification.

"No, I wanted to bring the whole thing out right," she averred, "because when I told Mr. Friedman he told me to tell the truth about everything, and I says to my boy, when I go there I want him with me to go and find that house, and we found it."

The cross-examination had been exhaustive. Yet the witness

[62]

did not seem tired. She still seemed eager. Wells paused for his own refreshment and exchanged a word with Cox. Was it worth going into new ground or retracing any of the old? The witness had been weakest in her description of Mabel Seymour. Wells decided to have another go at that subject, hoping to demonstrate that she was either resorting to imagination or was really unfamiliar with Mrs. Greer.

"How old was this woman, as you observed her at the time you took her in?" he resumed.

"She looked to me like twenty-four, twenty-five."

"How old were you?"

"Well, maybe I was a year older, or something like that, but I am not a very good judge, but I think she was that."

"What was the colour of the eyes of this girl, as you recall?"

"I can't remember. It is too long ago."

"Did you ever observe the colour of her eyes?"

"No. I always kept looking at her hair."

"What did you recall about her hair?"

"Well, like a chestnut brown."

"That is all you recall?"

"That is all—dark."

"Did this girl have long hair or short hair?"

"Sometimes it looked long, sometimes it looked short. She used to cut her hair once in a while, too."

"How did she use to wear her hair? Do you remember that?"

"Sometimes she wore it high up, like—you know. Years ago we used to have like a student bang and stuff that way."

"Did you observe her complexion?"

"Fair. She wasn't dark."

"Do you recall whether she had a dimple on her chin?"

"Who could remember all of that?"

"Do you recall whether she had any cleft on her lip?"

"Any what?"

"A cleft or depression on her lip, her upper lip."

"I never noticed anything on her lip. To me, she seemed to be very sweet and adorable. That is the way I found her."

"What was her weight at that time?"

"Well, I don't know, but I know she wasn't fat."

"Can you recall her weight fifteen years later when you saw her?"

"No, I don't know her weight. I never knew my own weight, either, till I got weighed lately."

Wells was satisfied. He was prepared to argue, when the time came, that Mrs. Sheppard had known no such person as Mabel Seymour. She may have had some such experience as she described with some woman, but if so the woman had not been Mabel Seymour Greer, in his opinion.

He had only one remaining interest in her—how she supported herself. Mrs. Sheppard's answer to that question was that up to seventeen years ago she had gone out with stationery and little novelty things. Now, she said, "I don't keep no business. I keep it with me, and if my friends want a pin I sell it to them."

Wells looked at Cox. With unspoken understanding the one sat down and the other stood up. The witness remained, ready for another encounter.

Cox started tentatively, "When did you first read about this case in the newspapers?"

"I think it was January sometime. I never keep a memory of anything. I started reading and then I got very interested."

"When you read it in the paper, what did you do about it?"

"I read every paper I got about it and when I seen the end of the story I says, 'Well, now, it is time for me to sit down and write a letter.'"

"When was that?"

"Oh, here some time ago."

"When?" Cox became sharp. "Please tell me, if you can."

"Listen, I am old," the woman pleaded. "I can't keep everything on my mind."

"Will you please answer the question, if you can?" His tone indicated no mercy.

"Only lately. It wasn't so long ago, but I never think of the month or the day or anything. I just read it."

"Are you testifying that you don't have any memory of anything?" the lawyer asked challengingly.

Emphatically the woman replied, "Oh, I got memories, but when I read the paper that settles it."

Cox took a breath. "You said this girl seemed to be about twenty-four or twenty-five years of age?"

"I am not a good judge, but she looked that way to me."

"How old were you then?"

"I must have been her age, too."

"How old were you?" he repeated impatiently.

"Well, I got married at——"

"How old were you? Please!" His tone now indicated exasperation.

"I guess about the same, because I am seventy-seven now."

"You don't know, do you?" the lawyer asked, as if the same observation might be made of all her statements.

"I told you I never remember any years or nothing like that" was the limited but final admission.

Cox stepped back to his place at the counsel table, glanced at his notes of the testimony given by the witness on her direct examination by Friedman and cross-examination by Wells, and then he embarked on his own close questioning on events in the house when Mabel Seymour supposedly stayed with Mrs. Sheppard, their conversations about the child and their trips on the road.

"Did she buy her own merchandise or did you buy that?" he asked.

"She bought her own and I bought my own," the witness explained, and added, "She offered to pay me for being in my home, and I told her, 'No, Mabel, you ain't got too much. You need what you got.'"

"Did she stay out overnight sometimes?"

"Nowhere, never."

"Always came back?"

"Always came back."

"Did she ever have any visitors?"

"Never."

"Just stayed in your happy family?"

"That is all."

"Then she went away in March, you say. Where did she go?"

"To New York. I got a card she arrived safe."

"Have you got the card?"

"Oh, my God! If I had everything . . ." the woman ejaculated.

Cox did not allow the exclamation to deter him. "Did she ever write anything else besides this card?"

"Nothing."

"Never heard from this girl that you had befriended again?"

"Never, until—let me see—Mannie was seventeen years old."

The lawyer was not going to accede to this manner of reckoning time and snapped out, "What year?"

"I don't recall," the woman answered, and then: "Wait a minute." After a moment's reflection she qualifiedly met the lawyer's terms and said, "I think it was in 1909 or something like that, I believe."

"Do you know it was 1909?" he demanded.

"Well, she told me she got married and that was 1909," she affirmed.

"Do you remember that it was 1909?"

"That I remember, when she came. That much I remember."

"You remember that?" Mocking incredulity marked the question.

"That I will always remember," she maintained.

Cox eyed the old woman sternly and detected the first signs of fatigue. He decided to bear down and let loose a bombardment of questions about Mrs. Greer's second appearance in Worcester.

"Weren't you surprised after fifteen years to see this woman walk in?" he asked tauntingly.

"I was thunderstruck when I seen her," was the acknowledgment.

"You were thunderstruck?"

"Oh, boy! Who ever expected to see her again?"

"Why were you thunderstruck?"

"I never believed that I would ever see Mabel again."

"Is that the only reason you were thunderstruck?"

"No. I felt—ooh, I got excited. I said, 'My God, what does this mean?'"

"And it was then you learned she was married?"

"She told me she married a very rich man, that she was happily married."

"Did you ask her the name of the man?"

"Oh, no. She wouldn't tell nobody."

"Did you ask her?"

"I did, but she wouldn't tell nobody."

"And you weren't interested in the name?"

"Well, it was her husband. She could do what she liked."

"Did you ever ask your friend Mae Schoell the name of the husband?"

"She didn't know it either. Mabel never told her, no more than she told me. She was living in fear. She didn't want no one to know. That is the answer."

The witness would have liked to make it the final answer, but Cox pressed on.

"Did this girl tell you when she was married?"

"Yes—1908."

"You remember that?"

"Yes."

"What year were you married?"

"I don't remember that, because my marriage——"

The explanation got no further before the lawyer broke in, "You don't remember when you were married, do you?"

A race was developing between lawyer and witness, with questions and answers in hot pursuit.

"My marriage paper got lost," she slipped in.

"But you remember when this girl was married?" he interjected.

"Well, she told it to me," she explained.

"That is the only year that you remember?"

"She told me——"

Cox broke in again, "But anything that happened to you, your son or daughter, the only year you remember——"

The race was getting feverish, and both lawyer and witness were talking at once.

"I ain't got the patience to keep all those things on my mind. I am old," she complained.

Ignoring the plea, the lawyer finished, "The only thing you have got the patience to keep on your mind is the year Mabel was married?"

"She was good to me. I will always love her."
"And you remember the year that she was married?"
"That is what she told me."
There was nothing more for either to say.

10

At the Bank

*   *   *   *   *

THE Fifth Avenue where Louis Greer strolled when the century was young is now a picture-book legend. The mansions have been replaced by towering structures where people live on top of one another in three- or four-room apartments. The old-world buildings which housed individual businesses have also disappeared in favour of the multiple accommodations of the skyscrapers. One of the old, so quietly dignified that its distinctiveness was hardly noticed, until recently occupied a corner at Forty-fourth Street.

It presented a façade on the avenue of sand-coloured stone, and on the street of red brick washed pink and smooth. The windows on the front were high-arched and flanked with fine Corinthian columns. The one toward the corner was bayed and latticed with heavy mullions, giving the outward appearance of an eighteenth-century counting-house. The thin handrail of brass on the iron railing along the steps leading to the recessed entranceway had been well polished by gloved hands. Their owners had been guided there by the light hanging from a strong iron chain and displaying on its front pane the gilt numerals 530-32, the address on the avenue of the Fifth Avenue Bank.

Here, in the inner hall with its high-vaulted ceiling and huge, square pillars, Louis Morris Greer came to bank as a young man, and as the years passed his balance grew. Here also, in her time, but in quarters reserved for the ladies, Mabel Seymour Greer came to deposit the gold pieces received by her husband as directors' fees and turned over to her as affectionate tokens. She loved the chamber so exquisitely designed for feminine clients—the gold-satin damask panels, the beige woodwork and fluted columns crowned with gold capitals, the satinwood furniture in informal arrangement—and she loved the petite, dark-haired, bright-eyed woman who presided over it.

The exceptional business acumen of Dorothy Armbruster has since been given the exceptional recognition of a vice-presidency of the bank. Mrs. Greer recognized it with an instinct she herself had for finance, an instinct well developed under the able tutoring of her husband over a decade before Dorothy Armbruster arrived on the scene. The older woman was already a familiar figure in the setting at that time. The gold pieces had mounted up to a tidy sum, and dividends and interest were accumulating on securities which her husband had set aside for her. It was under Miss Armbruster's guidance, however, that Mrs. Greer's growing interest in making money of her own came to fruition.

She found in the stock market occupation for her thoughts and outlet for her energies. She prospered. Indeed, she did so well that the fortune at stake in this lawsuit was mainly of her own making, Mr. Greer having left her only the income of his own estate. Her success earned for her from her appreciative husband the sobriquet of "Hetty", after the woman wizard of Wall Street, Hetty Green.

To the woman at the bank the ever-fresh enthusiasm of her client for business matters was both stimulating and rewarding. Miss Armbruster was the more interested and intrigued that the money-making was not a necessity or prompted by any apparent purpose or put to any apparent use. Here was a woman who would be expected to absorb herself in the social whirl. She had a spacious town apartment and a country house, rounds of entertainment and no financial limitations. She did not spend great sums on herself or on interests outside her home. Yet she was intent on creating wealth of her own. There was also a strange combination in the moods with which she applied herself to the task, baffling and beguiling to Miss Armbruster. She seemed to regard it as a game to be pursued in a playful spirit, yet also with a determination which evinced a passion. Miss Armbruster wondered also at the cloud of unexplained sadness that sometimes overcame the natural exuberance, and she had the feeling at times that her friend was being pursued or pushed by some deep force.

What she did not know was that every time Mabel Greer entered the bank and enjoyed its refined surroundings and atmosphere she thought of another bank and a quite different atmosphere—a cold, stone-domed room with no tables or chairs, just a number of cages where people stood in line to deposit or withdraw a pittance and where, one winter day so long ago, she had gone with all the money she had in the world, twelve dollars and fifty cents, to open her first bank account, only to withdraw half of it the next day and the other half four days later.

The friendship between the two women extended beyond the bank and frequent lunches to visits to the Armbruster home in Westchester, where Miss Armbruster lived with her family. On such occasions Miss Armbruster would observe a basic simplicity, an almost childlike quality in her friend. Saturday in the wintertime became her regular visiting day, and the visits were timed to the baking. Oven-fresh rolls and cakes were a delight to her. This indulgence was followed by an hour with Miss Armbruster's father, a minister, from whom she teased the morrow's sermon or to whose quiet talk she listened enthralled. She had a reverence for this man and contributed to his church although she did not attend the services. She was saddened by his death, and her floral tribute, a cross of lilies eight feet high, was a token of warm sentiment.

Miss Armbruster thought of all these things at the trial as she answered mechanically the questions put to her by the lawyers and imparted the information she had received from Mrs. Greer toward the end of her life.

"She told me," Miss Armbruster said, "that she had had a child prior to her marriage to Mr. Greer; that she was a very young girl—I think she said that she was sixteen—that she had had an affair with a young medical student, and this child was born and left in a boarding house and that she had never seen it again. She said, now that her attorney had the full story, she didn't have any more fear about it. She had given him all of the details, and she gave me very few. She was my friend and knew how badly I would feel——"

The answer was choked off at this point by an objection. How Miss Armbruster felt was immaterial to the lawsuit, as was the Mrs. Greer whom she had known and loved. Her feeling and knowledge might be interesting, even revealing of Mrs. Greer's character, but they were beside the point in issue—the identity of Mrs. Greer's son—and the Surrogate never let a case get off the track. So what Miss Armbruster cherished in her friend was kept outside the courtroom.

11

Raymond Armbruster—Defender
of the Will

*   *   *   *   *

R AYMOND ARMBRUSTER did not like court proceedings. As a lawyer he knew that the ultimate in legal matters was a court decision; that when men contended for their rights they had to go to court and have an impartial arbiter, judge or jury, hear the evidence and, out of a wisdom presumed from their office, find the truth and pronounce a judgment. He had respect for the judicial process. But it was laborious, tedious and time-consuming. And lawyers in the role of champions were not to his taste. He preferred an office practice, getting the facts in ordinary ways, and dealing with people in a non-adversary relationship.

Armbruster was a sociable person. He was tall, tanned, good-looking and easy of manner. Both men and women found him attractive, and he liked them as they liked him. His friends were his clients, and his clients were his friends. Among both clients and friends for fifteen years were Mr. and Mrs. Louis Morris Greer.

The friendship had grown out of Mrs. Greer's friendship with

Armbruster's sister, Dorothy, and the visits at the Armbruster home. On occasions when legal papers or advice were required, Mrs. Greer turned to Raymond Armbruster. But mostly their contacts were social, and seldom did the Greers give a dinner party at their Park Avenue residence, Voisin's or the Plaza when the handsome Armbruster was not among their guests.

He in turn equally enjoyed the company of the Greers, the keen intellect and urbanity of the man, the verve and charm of his beautiful wife. A striking figure she was. Armbruster often thought what a gorgeous girl she must have been, for even in her sixties her skin was lovely, her hair shone and her eyes danced.

Pleasant were the evenings spent in her company. Not so pleasant the hours spent in the witness chair, recalling the last time he saw Mabel Greer and accounting for the will he drew for her on that day. That was August 8, 1946, and two days later she was dead.

Friedman had called him as the claimant's witness, but eyed him coldly.

"Now, Mr. Armbruster, in preparing this purported will of August 8, 1946, how many conferences did you have with Mrs. Greer?" he asked.

The witness ignored the slur on his handiwork implicit in the question and answered directly, "I had a conference with Mrs. Greer on June 3, 1946, and another conference on August 7, 1946."

Picking up the statement which Armbruster had filed with the court when the will was filed—which Friedman had already made good use of in his opening and which he intended to revert to again and again—and brandishing it before the witness, Friedman said solemnly, "Mr. Armbruster, I am reading from your affidavit on file in this court. You state in that affidavit:

'On June 3, 1946, I had a conversation with Mrs. Greer in which she told me that when she was a young girl a child was born to her.' Is that statement correct?"

Wells rose and entered the objection that might be expected. The witness was on direct examination and the rule is that unless he turned out to be hostile to the party who called him the questioning could not take the form of a cross-examination. His prior statement might be used to contradict or impeach his testimony, but only after he had first been given the opportunity to testify to the facts and if his testimony turned out to be at variance with his prior statement. Wells was not going to allow Friedman to create the impression at the outset that Armbruster could not be trusted to state the facts fairly or that he required prodding.

The objection was sustained, the judge advising, "If you want to know what the conference was about, ask the witness. Then if he fails to testify in accordance with the affidavit, ask him to refresh his recollection by it."

Friedman had his own ideas of how he wished to proceed and spoke up. "I think, your Honour, I should be allowed with the witness, who is the attorney for the estate and a hostile witness——"

The drift of the argument was apparent to the perceptive judge, and there was no need to continue it. He made the decisive interruption. "I have not yet observed any evidence of hostility. When you develop that I will give you more freedom. Meantime, pursue the regular course."

Friedman reframed the question. "Mr. Armbruster, in this conversation you had with Mrs. Greer on June third, will you tell us what she said to you, if anything, with respect to a son that she had given birth to when she was a young girl?"

In straight recital the witness answered, "Mrs. Greer stated to me that when she was sixteen years of age she had gone to Boston, Massachusetts, to study music, that while there she met a young, attractive college student by the name of Willard Segur. At that time he was taking premedicine courses. He was a great athlete and a great football player. Mrs. Greer fell in love with him. Mrs. Greer stated that she had an affair with him and that a child was conceived. Rather than have an abortion she had gone to a private nursing home operated by an Irish lady; that the child was born at this private nursing home; that the doctors who delivered the child were Dr. Harvey Cushing and Dr. Derby, both of Boston; that at the time of the child's birth she signed the child over to the Irish lady in charge of the private nursing home for adoption; that she had never seen and never heard from the child or its father since the date of the child's birth. Mrs. Greer stated that she later learned that the father completed his medical courses and became the Chief Medical Examiner of the State of Massachusetts; that her child was reared as an adopted child by its father; that the father educated the child at the Fieldstone Preparatory School and at Dartmouth College. One evening in 1939, when she was preparing——"

Mention of 1939 indicated to Friedman that the witness was going to refer to Mrs. Greer's reading of Dr. Segur's death notice. He did not wish to get into that subject and interrupted the narration.

"Mr. Armbruster, please, I asked only what Mrs. Greer said to you regarding the birth of the child. If you have finished with that, I will ask you only to identify for future reference the notes you made of that conversation with Mrs. Greer."

The witness handed over the notes he had before him. With a nod to Wells, Friedman sat down to their perusal.

Wells picked up the thread where Friedman had cut it off.

"Did Mrs. Greer on that occasion tell you anything further than that which you have been permitted to testify to?" he asked.

"Yes, she did."

"Will you please tell us what further she said?"

The witness continued. "She said that one evening in 1939, when she was preparing to go to the theatre, she happened to pick up the New York *Evening Sun* and saw a death notice of Willard Segur and that he had left an adopted son."

"Other than by reference to the death notice of Dr. Segur did Mrs. Greer tell you how she had learned that her child had been adopted by Dr. Segur?"

"She did not."

"By the way," interjected Wells, "how did this conversation with Mrs. Greer start?"

"The conversation started with Mrs. Greer telling me how put out she was that Frank Reitman, her chauffeur, had left her, after all that she had done for him, how she had paid him and kept him in her employ during the war when they didn't have any car at all and how Mr. Greer had purchased a taxicab for Frank. Then she asked me if I had seen or heard from Frank Reitman recently. I told Mrs. Greer that the last time I had seen Frank Reitman was one evening when I was in the Army, was returning from Washington, D.C., I had taken a cab at the Pennsylvania Station and the cab driver happened to be Frank Reitman. She then asked, 'Did he tell you anything about me?' I answered that Frank Reitman advised me that he had left the employ of the Greers because he could not stand Mrs. Greer any longer. Then he asked me did I know that Mrs. Greer had a child, to which I replied that I did not. Frank then told me that one day when he was at the Piping Rock Club with Mrs. Greer a young man had approached him and exhibited a picture of Mrs. Greer and asked how Mr. and Mrs. Greers' health was. The boy had described himself as Willard Segur, Jr., the son of Mrs. Greer."

"When you told Mrs. Greer that, what did she say?"

"Mrs. Greer stated that was the reason she had sent for me, that she wanted to tell me a story. She then told me what I have already related, including the Piping Rock incident."

"In this conversation did Mrs. Greer identify the child by name?"

"She referred to the child as Willard Segur, Jr."

With this answer the subject of Armbruster's conversation with Mrs. Greer was closed as far as Wells was concerned. He turned to Armbruster's subsequent conversations with Harold Segur, starting with a telephone call to Segur in Worcester on the morning of August 14, 1946.

"What did you say and what did he say to you?" he asked.

Armbruster selected another set of notes from his portfolio and, placing them before him, responded, "I told Mr. Segur that I was the attorney for the Fifth Avenue Bank of New York, who had been named the executor in the last will of Mrs. Greer. I told him then that I had a few questions I would like to ask him, and asked him if he would mind answering them. Mr. Segur said he would be only too glad to. I then asked him his age. He told me he was forty-nine years of age. I then asked him who his father was. He said his father was Willard Segur, who had practised medicine at Enfield, Massachusetts, and had later moved to Ware, Massachusetts; that his father was a graduate of Princeton University and Dartmouth College School of Medicine; that his father was dead. I then asked him who his mother was. He stated that his mother was Mary Theresa O'Donnell, who had later married Dr. Segur; that she had been born in Provincetown, Massachusetts; that she had died in 1926. I then inquired of Mr. Segur if he had ever been to the Piping

Rock Club at Locust Valley, New York. Mr. Segur advised me that he had never been to New York City except once in his life, and at that time he had visited the World's Fair."

"When did you next contact Mr. Segur?"

"On the afternoon of August fourteenth."

"What did you say to him and what did he say to you then?"

Armbruster continued the narrative. "I told him that I had a few more questions I would like to ask him. Mr. Segur said, 'Go ahead.' I asked Mr. Segur where he was born. He stated that he was born in Boston, Massachusetts. I asked Mr. Segur when he was adopted. He stated that he could not give me the exact date, as he had the papers at home. He stated then that he was an illegitimate child, had been adopted by Dr. Willard Segur and Mary T. Segur; that the person consenting to his adoption was Mary Theresa O'Donnell. I then inquired of Mr. Segur where he had received his education. Mr. Segur told me he had graduated from Dean Academy and had attended Dartmouth College for one year."

"Did you discuss with him on that occasion an appointment?"

"I then asked Mr. Segur if it would be possible for me to see him, as he had advised me that he had all the papers relating to himself at his home. I made an appointment at that time to meet him at his home on the afternoon of August 15."

The witness was then called on to relate his conversation with Harold Segur at the latter's home in Worcester the following day.

"I asked Mr. Segur if he could tell me when and where he was born. Mr. Segur stated that he was born in the Lying-In Hospital, Boston, Massachusetts, February 26, 1887. I then asked Mr. Segur when he was adopted. Mr. Segur then took out an envelope and took a copy of the adoption papers from the envelope and read to me that he was adopted in 1901 on the petition of Dr. Willard B. Segur and Mary T. Segur; that at that time his name was Harold A. Baker, and by the adoption his name was changed to Harold A. Segur. I then inquired of Mr. Segur where the name 'Harold A. Baker' came from."

"What did he say to that?"

"Mr. Segur stated that he did not know; that he had spoken to one Nellie Howe, who was the wife of the Postmaster at Enfield, Massachusetts; that she was born in the same town where his adopted mother was born, Provincetown, Massachusetts, and that she had advised him that he was not the child of Mary Theresa O'Donnell, but that Mary Theresa O'Donnell had taken him at his birth for the purpose of blackmailing one Harold A. Baker, who was a prominent citizen about Boston, Massachusetts, and inducing him to marry her."

"What else did he or what else did you say at that point?"

"Mr. Segur then stated, 'Would you like to see a baby picture of me?' He then produced a baby picture of himself, with the longhand writing on it 'Harry A. Baker, born February 26, 1888,' with the numeral '1' drawn through the numeral '2,' making the date February 16, 1888. I then asked Mr. Segur why he had told me that he was born February 26, 1887, while here he had a photo of himself showing a date in 1888. Mr. Segur said, 'I might have been born that date, but I presume that was the date the photo was taken.' "

"What else was said?"

"Mr. Segur then told me that his mother had told him that the doctor who brought him into this world was Dr. C. A. Cliff."

"Did he tell you anything else? Did you ask him anything else?"

"I inquired of Mr. Segur about the discrepancy between our phone conversation and the conversation we held in his apartment as to his age. Mr. Segur asked me what I meant, and I told him, 'Over the phone you told me you were forty-nine years of age. Mrs. Greer told me that when she was sixteen she had borne this child. Mrs. Greer, I know, was sixty-five when she died, so I thought you might be her son. Now it shows that you are fifty-nine years of age. It would be quite impossible for Mrs. Greer to have had a child at the age of six!' "

"What did he say to that?"

"Mr. Segur said, 'Well, I was so excited when you phoned, that I might be going to learn my real parentage at last, that I might have said almost anything.' "

"Was anything further said on the subject of parentage?"

"Only that when Mary T. Segur had died in 1927, he had been appointed administrator of her estate, and that he had hired at that time an attorney in Boston to make a search regarding his parentage; that the search had proved fruitless."

The nod now was from Wells to Cox. Cox felt that there was little to add to what the other had brought out. He reverted briefly and pointedly to Armbruster's conversation with Mrs. Greer.

"After she finished telling the story," he asked, "did she say anything about whether Mr. Greer knew about her child or not?"

"She stated that she often started to tell Mr. Greer about her child, but that Mr. Greer would never permit her to tell it."

"Did she say why Mr. Greer would never permit her to tell it?"

"She stated that Mr. Greer told her the past that had gone on before they were married was a closed book as far as he was concerned."

"Did you ever again talk with Mrs. Greer about her son?"

"On August seventh, in the preparation of the will."

"What did she say on that occasion about her son?"

"She stated that she did not wish this child to receive one red cent of her money."

On this abrupt but final note Cox sat down.

Friedman felt that the time had now come when he could go after the witness in his own way. Two things he wanted to accomplish. One was to discredit the Reitman story and the alleged appearance of Mrs. Greer's son under the name of Willard Segur. Mrs. Greer had been so free in telling people about having a child by Dr. Segur when she was a young girl that Friedman guessed that Reitman had learned about it prior to the Piping Rock incident and had made up the Piping Rock story to scare Mrs. Greer. The other thing Friedman wanted to establish if he possibly could, because it was the mainspring of his case, was that Mrs. Greer learned of the adoption of her child by Dr. Segur prior to reading of his death in the newspaper, and that her statements about the adoption were not a mere supposition from what she had read in the newspaper.

Friedman fully realized that the case was in delicate and precarious balance on this point on which the decision would likely turn. The question really was: could Mrs. Greer's statements that her son was adopted by Dr. Segur be trusted?

Normally one could not ask for better evidence as to the identity of a child than a mother's declaration. And Mrs. Greer had made the most solemn statement of identification, her statement to her lawyer at the end of her life, practically a deathbed declaration. Yet the statement was open to the suspicion that Mrs. Greer did not know as a fact what she averred. How could she know it? That was a question which the judge would surely ask before he gave complete credence to her statement.

Wells had succeeded in the cross-examination of both Mrs. Jackson and Mrs. Tierney in raising a substantial doubt as to the reliability of Mrs. Greer's report to those witnesses concerning the adoption of her child. It was not until 1939, after reading the obituary of Dr. Segur and noting that he had left an adopted son, that Mrs. Greer had told either Mrs. Jackson or Mrs. Tierney that her son had been adopted by Dr. Segur. Mrs. Sheppard had given testimony which, if credited, would dictate a belief that Mrs. Greer surely knew that Dr. Segur had taken and adopted the child. But would the court accept Mrs. Sheppard as a credible witness? Friedman could not be sure.

Mrs. Greer had consistently stated that she had not heard from the child or its father since leaving the child with the woman who operated the boarding house or nursing home. Then how could she have learned that the child had been adopted by his father?

Friedman felt that he had found the answer to this all-important question, the key to the riddle, in Armbruster's notes of his June third conversation with Mrs. Greer and in Armbruster's statement filed with her will. It was with relish, therefore, that he undertook to extract from Armbruster the choice bits of evidence to support Segur's position.

First, however, he would undertake, with some expected co-operation from Armbruster, to lay the ghost of Piping Rock.

"Mr. Armbruster," he began, "do you recall my office associate, Miss Lilian Weinberg, calling to see you?"

"I do."

"Do you recall telling Miss Weinberg at that time that you felt that Frank Reitman was blackmailing Mrs. Greer?"

"I think I made mention to Miss Weinberg that others whom I had interviewed had said that to me."

"Yes. And didn't you tell her that you were of the same belief?"

"I don't recall whether I said that I felt the same way. I might have."

The witness was obviously being cautious on this delicate subject, but the impression given was clear enough and adequately served Friedman's purpose. He could now turn to his really important objective.

"Mr. Armbruster, do you recall testifying for Mr. Wells this morning that Mrs. Greer did not tell you how she learned of the adoption of her son?"

"I do."

"Was that answer correct?"

"It was."

"Permit me then," Friedman said acidly, "to refer you to your notes of your conversation with Mrs. Greer, and I read from page three of your memorandum: 'She kept in touch with the lady in charge of the nursing home and learned that the child was adopted by its father, Willard Segur.' Did you write that?"

"Yes."

"And you state that Mrs. Greer did not tell you from whom she learned of the adoption of her son?"

"I do."

"After having read this memorandum made by you?"

"I do."

"You are positive that she never told you that?"

"I am positive."

Friedman appeared incredulous. "Do you understand what I am asking you, sir?"

The witness was definite. "I do, and I am positive that she never told me that."

The judge had followed this exchange intently, fully sensitive to its import, and felt impelled to make inquiry.

"What did she tell you which led you to write the text which counsel read to you a little while ago?" he asked. "Read it into the record now. Let us see what you say she told you on the subject. What do your notes say?"

The witness replied, "My notes say, 'She kept in touch with the lady in charge of the nursing home and learned that the child was adopted by its father, Willard Segur, and was named Willard Segur, Jr.'"

The judge continued the interrogation. "Did Mrs. Greer say something which led you to make that note?"

"No, she did not, sir," the witness replied. "That is just the way I wrote it down hurriedly that afternoon, after I returned to my office."

"Did you write something in your memorandum respecting a matter which Mrs. Greer did not discuss with you?"

"No, I did not."

"Then what did she say to you which led you to write that note?" the judge asked firmly.

"She merely mentioned to me that she kept in touch with the lady in charge of the nursing home. Then later she told me she learned that the child had been adopted by its father, Willard Segur, and had been named Willard Segur, Jr."

"Is this person whom your note describes as the lady in charge of the nursing home the same person whom you have referred to as the 'Irish lady'?"

"Yes, sir."

Friedman was pleased with his excursion into Armbruster's notes, the more so that the judge had taken a hand in the questioning and pressed the witness. But he was not finished; there was another trump to play. He returned tchis favourite card, the Armbruster affidavit, the statement submitted to the court when the will was filed.

"Now, Mr. Armbruster," he said, "I will read to you from your affidavit sworn to September 5, 1946, wherein you state as follows, on page four——"

This was beginning to hurt, and Wells rose and repeated his earlier objection. This time the judge snapped out, "Overruled."

Continuing, Friedman read from the witness's prior statement: "Mrs. Greer had communicated with the person who operated the home at Boston and learned that the child later was adopted by his father, Willard B. Segur, who became a Medical Examiner in the State of Massachusetts. Later she read of the death of Dr. Segur in the New York newspaper."

"Is that statement correct?" Friedman asked.

"That statement is in my affidavit," the witness affirmed.

"Is it correct?" Friedman shouted.

"It is not correct that she learned from the lady in charge of the nursing home," Armbruster replied precisely.

"In other words," Friedman said triumphantly, "the affidavit is not correct?"

"The affidavit is correct," came the measured reply, "but I did not mean that interpretation to be placed on my statement in the affidavit. I meant that she kept in touch with the lady in charge of the nursing home; that later she learned of the adoption, but not from the lady in the nursing home."

"I see," Friedman said dryly, and added with due emphasis, "That is *your* interpretation of the statement made in your affidavit?"

"That is the way I intended it," the witness said calmly.

12

Erika Segnitz—Total Recall

*   *   *   *   *

IN THE trial of lawsuits it is wise to press home an advantage, and Friedman felt that on Armbruster's testimony he had the advantage on the issue of when Mrs. Greer learned of the adoption of her son. In other respects Armbruster's evidence had been damaging, particularly his testimony of his conversations with Harold Segur and Segur's statements that he had been born in the Boston Lying-In Hospital and that the doctor who had brought him into the world was a Dr. Cliff. Segur would deny making those statements when he took the witness stand, but Friedman had a sufficient appreciation of the value of notes made contemporaneously with an interview to doubt that the judge would believe what Armbruster, an attorney of standing, had recorded in his notes. Indeed, Friedman was relying heavily on those notes regarding Armbruster's conference with Mrs. Greer.

When it came to dealing with the subject of time and place of birth, Friedman could well argue that Segur did not and would not know when or where he was born, and that any statements made by him on that subject should be lightly regarded and not held against him. What the lawyer wanted at the moment was to follow up his newly gained advantage on the adoption point and clinch that. He was, intent on shoring up the foundation of his case—Mrs. Greer's own identification of her child as the adopted son of Dr. Segur—by showing that her knowledge of the adoption antedated her reading of the death notice of Dr. Segur in 1939. It was at this juncture, therefore, that he decided to call Erika Segnitz to the stand.

A statuesque woman, her blond hair pushed back under a trim hat, answered the call. She spoke distinctly in a contralto voice, but with a decided German accent and manner of expression.

She told the court that she had known Mrs. Greer since 1930, when they met as house guests of a mutual friend in the Berkshires, and that ever since that time they had been close friends.

"Coming down to a period in 1936, do you recall having a conversation with Mrs. Greer in the spring of that year at her home?" Friedman asked.

"Yes," Miss Segnitz said. "She called me up at my home at Lake Mohegan and said she wants to see me very much, if it would be possible."

"Then, when you were with Mrs. Greer at that time, what did she say to you and what did you say to her?"

"When I entered her bedroom, she greeted me as usual, 'Hello, Erika,' spoke as usual, with a very slow voice, and was happy to see me. She said, 'Come near to me, Erika. I want to talk to you. I feel very blue. I am very heartbroken. I want to tell you some secret, as I trust you very much. I know whatever I will tell you now you won't gossip as the rest of the society does.' I said, 'What is it, Mabel?' She said, 'Come close to me. Sit down on my bed, but don't kiss me today, because I have a cold.' Then she took my hand and she said, 'Erika, I tell you now a secret, and please cross your heart not to tell anyone about it, as I trust you and have all the confidence in you.' I said, 'Well, Mabel, I am your closest friend and you can trust me. I will tell nobody.' Then she told me, with tears in her eyes, very heartbroken and upset, 'Erika, I have a son born out of wedlock.' I said, 'Well, Mabel, where is your son?' She said, 'Oh, near by in Boston.' I said, 'Who is the father?' She said, 'He is a doctor.' I said, 'Where is he living?' 'Some place by Boston in Massachusetts,' she said, and she was crying. I didn't want to ask too many questions. I said, 'What is the name of the father?' She said, 'Willard Segur.' Then I said, 'Can I not arrange any meeting?' as she wants to see her son very much. I said, 'Why do you not tell Mr. Greer about it?' She cried, 'Oh, it is impossible. It can't be done. You know, Erika, men are funny.' I said, 'Mabel, whatever I can do for you, let me know, because I love to see you happy.' I didn't ask her further questions because she got so upset."

Somewhat breathlessly the witness came to a stop.

"Excuse me a second," Friedman interjected. "Did you ask her in that conversation what happened to the boy?"

"Yes. She said the father adopted the son."

Friedman paused and then asked, "During the period from 1936, when you had this conversation with Mrs. Greer, up to the last time you spoke to her, did she ever speak to you about the boy again?"

"Very much so, yes."

"Do you remember a conversation in 1939, some time in February of that year?"

"Yes," the witness said, and she proceeded to describe the occasion. "I had just returned from Europe. I sent her a cablegram from the ship that I have arrived, so she looked me up

in the Hotel Dorset, where I usually took my place. She came
to me, as usual, with red roses, my favourite flowers."

"What did she say to you at that time about her son?"

"She said, 'Recently I heard that the father of my son Harry
died. Now I am really lost and I don't know what to do, as I'd
like to see him and I'd like to see him happy and well off, but
I don't want to trouble you today. Don't let us talk about it
further.'"

With evident satisfaction Friedman said, "That is all."

The impact of this testimony was not lost on either Wells
or Cox. They could not laugh it off as they might the testimony
of Mrs. Sheppard as that of an eccentric or busybody. Here was
an altogether responsible woman who undoubtedly had been a
close friend of Mrs. Greer and had no motive to falsify. It
would not do to employ the attack on her that had been made
on Jennie Sheppard and attempt to show that the whole story
was a fabrication. The witness might be mistaken as to dates or
details, and perhaps doubts could be cast on the reliability of
her memory, but her honesty could hardly be questioned or
her destruction as a witness hoped for. The cross-examination,
therefore, would have to take the course of questioning and
testing her memory, rather than an all-out attack on her credibility.

First Wells asked how she placed the time of her 1936 conversation with Mrs. Greer. She placed it, she said, with reference
to a conference with her attorney about her application for
citizenship, for the day that she saw Mrs. Greer was a day that
she came into town to see her attorney about her application
for citizenship. She also placed the date with reference to her
marriage, which had taken place only shortly before.

Some doubt was raised as to whether a conference with her

attorney could place the date, as the witness acknowledged that she had several conferences with her attorney about her citizenship between 1935 and 1940, when she became a citizen. The date of her marriage, January 12, 1936, could hardly be questioned, however, and she remained definite that the conversation she had with Mrs. Greer, in which she was told of the birth and adoption of the child, was about two months after her marriage.

Miss Segnitz admitted that the name of the child was not mentioned until the meeting after her return from Europe in February 1939, which was after Mrs. Greer had learned of the death of Dr. Segur. But she was definite that Mrs. Greer had then referred to the child as "my son Harry."

Wells closed his interrogation of the witness by bringing out that she had been a German citizen and lived in Hamburg before coming to this country in 1930; that she had been a movie actress in Germany but had not continued in that profession in this country; that she was now divorced and living on an alimony income.

Cox in his turn delved into the witness's meetings with Mrs. Greer, which had been frequent over the years. He forced the admission that she could not detail other conversations by date as she did the two conversations testified to, but he received repetitive answers that Mrs. Greer constantly referred to her son and expressed a desire to see him and do something for him and a great unhappiness that she was unable to arrange it for fear Mr. Greer would discover her secret.

Friedman remained satisfied with the testimony elicited and felt that there was no need for additional explanation or clarification by redirect examination. He decided to trust his fortune further, however, by inquiring as to Miss Segnitz's impression of Mrs. Greer's age. He was smarting under the point so emphatically made by Armbruster that a woman born in 1881 could not have a child born in 1887 or 1888. He was ever anxious to challenge the record of Mrs. Greer's age, and this he could do only through the testimony of people who had known Mrs. Greer and were qualified to express an opinion of her age.

Miss Segnitz proved equally rewarding on this score. She stated that Mrs. Greer appeared to be about sixty in 1930, which would have made it altogether possible for her to have had a child in 1887 or 1888.

Harold Segur—Contradictions

* * * * *

THE stage was now set for the appearance of Harold Segur. Friedman had arranged the presentation of his evidence so that practically all his proof would be in before Segur took the stand. He wished to relieve his client of carrying the burden of the case, to present him not in the role of a claimant but rather as one on whom the right descended. In fact, there was little that Segur could add in support of his position except his honest countenance and manner, and the sympathy engendered by the way he had been drawn into the proceedings. He would certainly appear as a deserving person.

Friedman knew that he would have to call Segur to explain his waiver of all rights in the Greer estate and his application to be relieved of that waiver and for permission to assert a child's claim against the estate. He knew also that Segur would have to contradict certain prejudicial admissions attributed to him by Armbruster. Beyond that, little purpose could be served by calling him except to submit him for judicial observation. He could give his understanding of his birth date, and that positively, on the basis of what he had been told within the family in which he was raised, but he could really know nothing of his parentage or date and place of birth. Indeed, it would be Friedman's final argument that no one knew these facts, but that Segur answered Mrs. Greer's description of her child, and that the very absence of other proof of parentage made it likely that the child adopted by Dr. Segur was his child by Mabel Seymour.

The man who took the witness stand had a fine face, frank eyes that looked through silver-rimmed spectacles, grey hair and a well-modulated voice. He spoke softly and answered simply all questions to the point, a virtue much to be desired in a witness. As he sat in the witness chair he appeared to be about sixty years of age.

"Mr. Segur, what is your first recollection of your early childhood?" Friedman asked.

"The earliest recollection that I can remember," the man stated, "is living with my foster-mother, Mary Theresa O'Donnell, in a house near a fire-engine station in Boston. It was sort of a boarding house where a lot of women lived. We all ate at the same table."

"Do you have any other recollection of your early childhood?"

"Yes. I can remember being taken by my foster-mother to visit Dr. Segur in a hospital in Boston. My next recollection is moving to Enfield, Massachusetts, when my foster-mother married Dr. Segur in 1895."

The lawyer went directly to the question of age. "When were you born, Mr. Segur?"

"February 16, 1888" was the precise reply.

Friedman took from an envelope which he held in his hand a photograph, an ivory-tone print on pasteboard, the picture of

a young child in a dress and high-button shoes seated snugly
on a fur rug. Segur identified it as a baby picture of himself.
There was written at the bottom of the picture, in a handwriting which he could not identify, the words "Harry A. Baker,
born Feb 26th, 1888" with a numeral "1" drawn through the
"2" in 26th, making it "Feb 16th, 1888."

The lawyer then handed the witness a paper, the petition of
Willard B. Segur and Mary T. Segur, his wife, for the adoption
of Harold Alfred Baker, described as a foundling of unknown
parentage, born at the Boston Lying-In Hospital on February
16, 1887. The petition recited that the child had been taken at
birth by Mary T. Segur and given her family name and had
since remained under her care and since her marriage under the
joint care of Dr. and Mrs. Segur. The petition was dated July
18, 1901, and was signed by Willard B. Segur and Mary T.
Segur, and at the bottom, after the printed legend—"I, the
child above named, being over the age of fourteen years, hereby
consent to the adoption"—was signed in a schoolboy's hand,
"Harold Alfred Baker."

"Mr. Segur," Friedman inquired, "is that your signature at
the bottom of that paper?"

"Yes, sir, it is."

"Where did you sign that paper?"

"In the living room of my home in Enfield."

"Who was present when you signed it?"

"The gentleman that had the paper, and Dr. Segur and myself."

"Was that the first time you heard the name 'Baker' mentioned with respect to yourself?"

"It was, yes, sir."

"Were you told why you were signing that paper at that
time?"

Baby picture of Harold Segur

"Yes, sir. The man that had the paper told me that when I was a baby I was brought up under the name of Harold A. Baker, but my name was to be changed to Harold A. Segur."

"When you signed that, did you read any portion of that paper?"

"No, I didn't."

"How old were you at that time?"

"Thirteen."

The judge asked for the paper and appeared to scan it with one eye while scrutinizing the witness with the other. It was not difficult to read his thoughts. The law permitted a child of fourteen to consent to his adoption. For a younger child, the law required the appointment of a special guardian to consider the child's interests and consent to his adoption. According to the adoption paper, Harold Segur was fourteen at the time and qualified to consent to his own adoption, and this statement of his age was supported by the stated date of his birth, February 16, 1887. Obviously Segur was now trying to get away from the birth date given in the adoption paper. And in this he was supported by the baby picture with its 1888 birth date.

The year's difference itself would be of no significance, except as a later birth date might help somewhat in arguing that Mrs. Greer could have been the mother of the child. But if Segur could throw doubt on the veracity of the statement of his birth date in the adoption paper, he could equally challenge the correctness of the stated place of birth, the Boston Lying-In Hospital. And that was important, for Mrs. Greer had consistently stated that her child was born in a boarding house or nursing home, not in a hospital.

The judge felt the mystery deepening rather than lifting through the documents. Here were three dates—what was the significance of the difference between them? The adoption paper gave a birth date of February 16, 1887. The baby picture gave a birth date of February 26, 1888, corrected to February 16. Was it accidental or a mere mistake at one time or the other that the year was recorded differently on the picture and in the adoption paper? And what of the change of date on the picture? Someone at some time had deliberately altered the day. If this represented a correction, so that the February 16 date could be accepted, it meant also that 1888 was the correct year, or at least that someone consciously addressing himself to the subject and presumably intent on accuracy had found what he thought was a mistake in the day but not in the year on the picture. But to add to the confusion, the judge remembered that Armbruster had testified that Segur had told him that he was born on February 26, 1887—so there were four dates to choose from.

The questions raised in the judge's mind were not answered by the further questions Friedman put to the witness. Instead of pursuing or asking any accounting for the discrepancy between the picture and the paper, Friedman asked his client to tell of his living in Dr. Segur's household and of his schooling at Enfield, at high school in Ware, Massachusetts, where the family had moved, at boarding school from which he graduated in 1908, and for a year at Dartmouth. At each stage the lawyer inquired how old Segur then was and received a categorical answer in accord with an 1888 birth date.

In 1907, the witness said, Dr. Segur and Mary T. Segur were divorced. Mrs. Segur left the house and he stayed with the doctor. He never saw his foster-mother again. She passed away in 1927.

He told next of his employment, which since 1935 had been as Employment Manager of the Pullman Standard Car Manufacturing Company in Worcester. The questioning then turned to his conversations with Armbruster, the first over the telephone on the morning of August 14, 1946. The call was made by Armbruster to Segur at his office.

"I will ask you," Friedman said, "to relate that conversation between yourself and Mr. Armbruster, as best you can."

In straight narrative the witness answered. "Mr. Armbruster asked me if I was Harold A. Segur. I said 'Yes.' He asked me if I was the adopted son of the late Dr. Willard B. Segur. I said 'Yes.' Then he identified himself as Mr. Armbruster, a lawyer connected with the Fifth Avenue Bank in New York, and he wanted to know if he could ask me a few questions. I told him 'Yes.' He asked me if I had ever heard of anybody by the name of Mabel Seymour Greer. I told him I never had. He asked me if I had ever been to some beach on Long Island. I don't remember the name of the beach. I told him 'No.' He asked me how old I was. I told him I was.between fifty-eight and fifty-nine. He wanted to know, if he had any further questions, if there would be any objection to his calling me at my office, that he had some information that he would tell me later. I.told him I had no objections."

"Did you have a second telephone conversation with him on that same day, August 14, 1946?"

"I did."

"Will you please tell us that conversation?"

"Mr. Armbruster identified himself, asking me if I could come to New York at his expense. I told him I couldn't leave my work. He wanted to know, if he came to Worcester, if he could see me. I told him at any time. He asked me if it would be convenient to come up the next day and at what time. I told him he could come up any time after five-thirty. He asked me what my street address was, and I told him 12 Auburn Street,

[99]

and he said he had some very important information and that he was sure that he could prove to me that Dr. Segur was my own father, and that he would see me the next evening."

"Mr. Segur," Friedman addressed the witness, employing a tone calculated to give emphasis to what was to follow, "you were in court here when Mr. Armbruster testified?"

"Yes, sir," the witness replied.

With rising voice Friedman put his next questions. "Mr. Armbruster stated that during the first telephone conversation with you, you told him that you were forty-nine years of age. Did you tell him that?"

"I did not, sir," the witness replied emphatically.

"Mr. Armbruster also testified that during this first conversation you said that your mother was Mary Theresa O'Donnell. Did you tell him that?"

"I did not," came the answer. "I told him that Mary Theresa O'Donnell was my foster-mother, but not my real mother."

"In this second telephone conversation that you had with him, who was present in your office?"

"My secretary."

"Mr. Armbruster testified that during that second telephone conversation you told him you were an illegitimate child. Did you so state to him in that telephone conversation?"

"Absolutely no," the witness replied with some heat. "I would not make that statement in front of a girl, anyway."

"On August 15, 1946," Friedman resumed in normal voice, "did Mr. Armbruster call to see you at your home?"

"He did."

"Will you tell us as near as possible the conversation and what took place at the visit of Mr. Armbruster at your home? Take it easy."

The witness, who had moved forward to the edge of the chair

and arched his back at the first indication of the question, relaxed at the admonition of his counsel and deliberately began his long answer.

"I don't know as I can give it in sequence—but I can give the substance. He called at my home somewhere around seven o'clock, and I met him at the front door and we went upstairs, and Mr. Armbruster told me that he had some very important information for me, but before he could give it to me there were some questions he wanted to ask me. He asked me when I was born. I told him February 16, 1888. He asked me where I was born. I told him Boston, Massachusetts. He asked me where I went to school and I told him the different schools. I don't recall whether I gave him the years or not. I think I did. He asked me where I worked after I left Dartmouth. I told him that I worked for a while in a restaurant in Springfield before getting a permanent job. He asked me the life history of Dr. Segur. He asked me about my family, how many children I had. I told him I had four boys. Then I think I asked him why he was asking all these questions and hadn't given me any information, and he told me that I had been very co-operative and that he would tell me the reason.

"He read a paper he took from his portfolio to the effect that Mrs. Greer about two months prior to her death had confided to him that when she was about sixteen years of age she had given birth to a boy in Boston and the father of that boy was Willard B. Segur, who was a premedic student at the time, and that she had found out afterwards that Dr. Segur had brought me up and adopted me. In the course of the conversation he asked me if Dr. Segur wasn't a very prosperous doctor, and I told him he was. He also read to me a statement that had been given him by a chauffeur named Frank—I think it was Riceman —about some man approaching him at some club and representing himself to be Mrs. Greer's son. Mr. Armbruster stated at the time that he didn't believe this story, because there had been several cases in the past where people had impersonated themselves as relatives in order to obtain an estate. He then took a copy of Mrs. Greer's will and read it to me—read part of it to me, and then handed me the paper and told me I might read it if I wished. I glanced through the paper. I didn't read it thoroughly. He stated to me that Mrs. Greer had not mentioned me in her will because she felt that when Dr. Segur died he was a very prosperous doctor and had amply taken care of me.

"He then told me that I, of course, had a right to contest the will, as an heir, but that it would involve tremendous expense, it might take many years of court proceedings, that in the end I might not get anything, and that it would cause a lot of publicity and notoriety, both to myself and family and to Dr. Segur and to Mrs. Greer, but that if I wished to sign a waiver releasing any claim to the estate, that he would guarantee me that there would be absolutely no publicity. On the strength of Mr. Armbruster's statement that there would be no publicity, I signed a waiver, although I told him at the time that I could certainly use the money, but I would do everything in the world to protect the name of my family, of Dr. Segur and Mrs. Greer. Mr. Armbruster then produced two copies of waivers, and I signed my name to both copies at my home.

"Mr. Armbruster then looked at me and said, 'I am perfectly satisfied that you are the right man, but the only question is the age of Mrs. Greer.' I asked him what he meant by the age of Mrs. Greer, and he said she was reported to be sixty-five at the time of her death and couldn't have been my mother if that was her age. I replied by reminding him that according to what Mrs. Greer had told him, she was sixteen and Dr. Segur was a premedic student when I was born, and I pointed out that Dr. Segur took his premedic courses at Princeton, graduating in 1889, so if Mrs. Greer was sixteen at that time she was much older than sixty-five when she died."

The recital completed and the strain on memory eased, the witness seemed relieved. Friedman allowed him only a moment's respite, however, before resuming. The lawyer then drew from his client in rapid succession denials that he had told Armbruster that he was born in the Boston Lying-In Hospital or that he was born on February 26, 1887, or that Dr. Cliff had brought him into the world or that Nellie Howe had said that Mary Theresa O'Donnell had taken him at birth for the purpose of blackmailing one Harold A. Baker. He acknowledged mentioning Nellie Howe to Armbruster, but only as a person who had told him, when she learned of his adoption, that she was very pleased because she always knew that Mary Theresa O'Donnell was not his mother. He also acknowledged mentioning Dr. Cliff to Armbruster, but only as one who had treated him for abscesses in his ears when he was a child.

"Did Mr. Armbruster speak to you or did you tell him anything regarding your living with the doctor after the doctor and Mrs. Segur were divorced?" the lawyer asked.

"I remember," the witness replied, "I told him that at the time that the doctor and Mrs. Segur separated—were going to separate—that the doctor called me into the house and told me the conditions were such that he and Mrs. Segur couldn't get along any longer, they were going to separate. He said I was old enough to know my mind, whether I wished to go with her or stay with him. I told him that by all means I was going to stay with him. He told me at that time that he was awfully glad that I made the decision as I did. He wanted me to always remember that blood was thicker than water."

After a pause to let the full force of this statement sink in, Friedman asked his last question.

"Just one thing more, Mr. Segur. Do you know the nationality of Mary Segur?"

"Well, her name was Mary Theresa O'Donnell, so I am pretty sure she was Irish, and I know when she died she was buried from the Catholic Church. I am pretty sure she was of Irish extraction."

14

Harold Segur—Birthday in Dispute

* * * * *

WELLS asked for a short recess before taking up the cross-examination. He wished to collect his thoughts and order the course of his questioning. He felt no antagonism for Segur and had no desire to give him a raking examination. He liked and even admired the man whose claim he was opposing. Segur was obviously a man of fine character and sensibilities. He had not bargained for the position he was in. He had been entirely willing, even anxious, to forgo this chance at riches, and certainly was no impostor faking a claim. His claim was natural enough, and having undertaken to prove it, he had, Wells thought, merely been carried away by a growing enthusiasm and inclined to remember only the facts favourable to his case.

Wells considered again going over the ground of Segur's conversations with Armbruster and the contradictions between the two, but there seemed no good reason for doing that. He thought that the judge would be more impressed with Armbruster's testimony from his notes, made at the time of the conversations, than by Segur's denials made considerably later and after reflection. Date and place of Segur's birth were the crucial facts, and Wells decided that he would strike right at the heart of the matter.

"Mr. Segur," he began, "you testified on direct examination by Mr. Friedman that you were born on February 16, 1888, but you were not asked the source of your knowledge as to that birth date. What makes you think you were born on that day?"

"Dr. and Mrs. Segur both told me that I was born February 16, 1888, and then the baby picture shows that date," the witness answered.

"Let us take the baby picture first," Wells said, picking it up from the counsel table and holding it for Segur's attention. "When did you first see that picture, and how did it come into your possession?"

Second |

"It was after the doctor's death, and the then Mrs. Segur was cleaning up and found the picture among some papers and gave it to me."

"That would be in 1939, wouldn't it?"

"Yes, sir."

"Who told you that was your photograph pictorialized on this picture?"

"Nobody actually told me, sir, but Mrs. Segur—"

Wells interrupted firmly, "Nobody actually told you, is that right?"

"That's right."

Advancing toward the witness and handing him the baby picture, the lawyer inquired, "Do you know who put that numeral '1' over the '2'?"

"No, sir, I do not."

"Was it on there when you first saw it?"

"When it was given to me, it was on there."

"Did you ever make any inquiry to find out who put the '1' over the '2'?"

"No, sir."

"Now we will turn," Wells continued, "to what Dr. and Mary Segur had to say about your birth date. I show you your adoption paper and ask whether you can identify the signatures of Willard B. Segur and Mary T. Segur thereon."

"I am absolutely sure of Willard B. Segur's signature," the witness replied, "but I don't think I ever saw Mary T. Segur's signature."

"You know now, do you not, that Willard B. Segur and Mary T. Segur stated that your birthday was February 16, 1887? Isn't that right?"

"It shows on there, yes, sir" had to be the answer.

"Is it your position," Wells asked, "that Dr. Willard B. Segur was falsely stating your age at the time he signed that document?"

"I don't know, sir" was all the witness could say.

Wells spread his net.

Under his questioning, Segur testified that at the time of his foster-mother's death in 1927, he retained a lawyer to represent him as administrator of her estate. The lawyer, Mr. Henry Wise of Boston, had previously represented Mary Segur.

"At or about that time you spoke to Mr. Wise concerning your parentage, did you not?"

"I asked him if Mrs. Segur had ever mentioned to him anything about my parentage, and he said she had not."

"Didn't you ask Mr. Wise to make an investigation concerning your parentage?"

"No. Mr. Wise volunteered that if he could get any information he would advise me."

"He spoke to you later concerning that investigation, didn't he?"

"Yes, sir."

"What did he tell you at that time?"

"He told me he hadn't made any progress, couldn't tell me who my father and mother were."

Wells was ready to close in.

"Didn't he tell you that he had found a record in the Lying-In Hospital, Boston, Massachusetts? Did he or didn't he?"

"Yes, he had found a record," the witness was compelled to say, but added defensively, "but he didn't say it was a record of me."

"What did he say with respect to that record?" the lawyer pursued.

"He told me that he had been to Lying-In Hospital and that he had found a record of a birth of a child, and if I would send him five dollars he would have the attendant or clerk at the hospital give me a copy of it."

"Thereafter you did obtain a copy of those records, didn't you?"

"He sent me a copy, or a letter, rather—sent me a letter."

"What is your best recollection, Mr. Segur, as to the contents of that letter?"

"It seems to me," the witness said falteringly, "it said there was—I don't remember whether it said a child or a son—born to an Addie Weston. I can't, without seeing the record, refresh my memory, but I know it said something about Addie Weston."

"Did he mention anything other than the name Addie Weston?" the lawyer asked suggestively.

Indefinitely the witness answered, "I think there was some date of birth there, but I don't remember what it was offhand."

Definitely the lawyer rejoined, "Would it refresh your recollection if I told you that the date referred to was February 26, 1887?"

"No, sir, it wouldn't," the witness replied.

Obviously he did not recall, or would not recall, the contents of the letter. It made no difference to Wells. He had interviewed the lawyer Wise and had seen a copy of the letter. All he cared to do at the moment was to test Segur, and in the process he could not resist teasing him.

"Was it the year 1887?" he asked.

"I don't remember that offhand," Segur maintained.

"It was a date different, wasn't it, from 1888?"

"I don't remember, sir. I am pretty sure there was a date on there," the witness conceded qualifiedly, "but I don't remember it now."

The testing went on.

"Did he mention the name Mary O'Donnell appearing on those records?"

"I don't remember it, sir."

"You don't remember that?"

"I can't remember that."

"Did he mention the name L. A. Cliff appearing on those records?"

"I can't seem to recall it. I don't remember that letter exactly."

"But you do remember Addie Weston's name appeared in the letter, is that right?"

"Yes, there was an Addie Weston."

With that much of an admission Wells closed his cross-examination. Cox expressed his approval and satisfaction by sitting silent.

Friedman, for his part, wished a final word on the issue of the birth date and also to take the edge off the impression created by Wells's excursion into the Wise letter and to explain why his client had appeared so indefinite about it.

"Did you ever have any birthday parties as a child?" he asked.

"Yes, sir, I did."

"Do you remember on what birthdays they were?"

"I remember the first party I ever had was when I was ten years old."

"On what day of the month was that celebrated?"

"February sixteenth."

"Why do you remember that birthday in particular?"

"Because the doctor gave me the first watch I ever owned at that particular party."

"Did you have any subsequent birthday parties?"

"I had a birthday each year after that until I got through with grammar school."

"On what day of the month were those celebrated?"

"Always on February sixteenth, sir."

Turning to the subject of the Wise letter, Friedman inquired, "After you received the letter from Mr. Wise, did you speak to Mr. Wise?"

"I spoke to him about the letter," the witness readily acknowledged.

"What did Mr. Wise tell you?"

"Mr. Wise told me that was the only record he could find, but he didn't think it applied to me."

That was all. Harold Segur left the witness stand, the courthouse, and New York. He left his fate in the hands of his vigorous lawyer and the inscrutable judge.

15

Speculation

* * * * *

WITH the conclusion of the examination of Segur, Friedman rested his case. It was now up to Wells and Cox to introduce any evidence they might have to counter the Segur showing. First, however, they made the usual motion to dismiss the claim on the ground that Segur had not made a sufficient showing to warrant going on with the case.

The judge made short shrift of this. "No," he said, "the inquiry must go on."

This required an application from the attorneys for time in which to conduct the inquiry. Obviously time was needed. In view of the court's ruling, they could not rest on the infirmities in the case so far made out by Segur. They would have to go forward on their own and prove that Harold Segur was not Mrs. Greer's child or at least raise such overriding doubts that in the end the Surrogate would have to decide that Segur had not sustained the burden of proof.

The request for an adjournment was reasonable. This was not an ordinary case to which the lawyers could come fully prepared at the start. Despite diligent search in every indicated direction, the threads of information going back sixty years were tenuous. They were hard to pick up and even harder to follow. None yet discovered had led home. The hope was that if enough could be pursued, they might converge at some point which would be recognizable as the truth.

It was fortunate for Wells and Cox that the case was being tried before a judge without a jury. A jury case cannot be interrupted with adjournments to allow lawyers to extend their search for evidence. But a judge, whose service is continuous and who is accustomed to staggering cases, is able and willing for a good reason to allow adjournments in cases being tried before him alone.

Friedman interposed no objection. While he preferred to go on without interruption, he knew that the request for an adjournment was in order and would be granted. He felt also that his case would be stronger in the judge's eyes if the opposition was given every opportunity to marshal evidence and was still unable to destroy his client's claim.

The best Wells and Cox could do would be to show that someone else was the child. Wells was not anxious to do this, however, as he did not care to knock down one claimant against the will he was endeavouring to sustain only to raise another. Cox was in a more open position. He didn't so much care whether another claimant was developed or not. He was intent on learning all that could be discovered. If Segur could be eliminated and nothing more was uncovered, then he could wage the will contest on his own for the benefit of the state. If someone else could be shown to be the child, that would surely eliminate Segur, and Cox would still have attractive alternatives. If that someone else had not survived Mrs. Greer, Cox would still have the right to contest the will. If the someone else had survived Mrs. Greer and should come into his inheritance, Cox would be the agency through which this was accomplished and the court would rightly award him a good fee from the estate for his contribution to its proper administration.

But there were no indications of the existence or identity of any other child, and the most that the lawyers could reasonably expect to do was to cast further doubts on Segur's claim.

One thing they felt they had strongly in their favour which they intended to harp on was Mrs. Greer's age. Not only did her application for a marriage licence show her to have been an age which would have made it quite impossible for her to have been Harold Segur's mother, but other records which they could produce would fortify the point.

There was another thing, the product of the extensive research already made into the background of Harold Segur and of his foster-mother, Mary Theresa O'Donnell Segur. It was information of a kind which would not qualify for admission as evidence in a court—hearsay, a statement made by one not available to testify and without any assurance that she knew whereof she spoke. Nevertheless, it was the kind of a statement which a lawyer might believe indicative of the truth and which sticks in his mind as significant.

Mary T. Segur had led a chequered life. Wells and Cox had traced it back as best they could. Their principal source of information was her own story, told thirty years earlier, when, distressed and distracted, she had been admitted as a patient in the Massachusetts State Hospital at Medfield. There a personal-history statement was taken and preserved. She told of an unhappy childhood, of being put to work at an early age, of marrying Mr. Baker, who was very kind to her and with whom she had been very happy until his death, and of meeting Dr. Segur some years later and marrying him in April 1895. With

Dr. Segur she had been unhappy and, according to her account, one would wonder how the marriage had lasted the twelve years they were together. The marriage had been doomed from the start, she said, because she had learned within two months that her husband was living under the name of Dr. Montclaire with a woman by the name of Seymour on Springfield Street, Boston.

"Seymour, Springfield Street, 1895" was a refrain that ran through the minds of the two lawyers. Was this the ranting of a mad woman or the truth revealed when inhibitions were removed? If not the truth, wherever would Mrs. Segur have come upon the name Seymour and connected it with her husband? This was the test that morally satisfied the lawyers, although legally the information was not probative.

If the affair between Mabel Seymour and Dr. Segur had been current in 1895, it was still possible that it had dated back to 1887 or 1888 and that Harold Segur was their offspring—but quite unlikely, the lawyers thought. Much more likely that any child born of this arrangement had a birth date closer to 1895. That would also better fit Mrs. Greer's professed age and her description of a child born to her in her early teens. Further, the coincidence of Mary Theresa O'Donnell adopting Mabel Seymour's child by Dr. Segur and then marrying Dr. Segur herself almost exceeded the conceivable—unless, as the devil's advocate within the lawyers kept suggesting, the man Mary Theresa succeeded in blackmailing into marrying her had not been Baker but Dr. Segur, and the instrumentality had been his child by Mabel Seymour.

Enough, however, of imagination running riot and speculation leading nowhere, they decided, as they tried to cast out of mind the inadmissible in favour of pursuing another avenue of inquiry opened up by the case so far. That was the Boston

Lying-In Hospital, where, according to his adoption papers, Harold Segur had been born.

Then, also, there was the great uncharted field of Mrs. Greer's life. The curtain was drawn across the years prior to 1908, but chinks might be found in it and glimpses caught which might aid in the search for her heir. There was always the hope that, as a Jennie Sheppard had appeared for Friedman, some old friends or acquaintances of bygone years might come forward and contribute something to the solution of the puzzle. Friedman was even hopeful that any further discoveries might favour his side.

The judge granted the application for an adjournment and said to all the attorneys, "There must be a decisive answer to this case. Even at this late date there must be some persons or some records that will make certain the truth. It is up to you gentlemen to find them. While you have divergent interests you are all in the case together and should co-operate to gather all the evidence you can and to find the truth."

Accordingly, the hearings were adjourned for six weeks, until June 25, 1947, and the lawyers went on their mission.

16

Birth in a Hospital

* * * * *

SO IT came about that on the eleventh day of June in the year 1947, the three attorneys gathered in the office of the director of the Boston Lying-In Hospital and examined the director, Dr. Wilson W. Knowlton, and the record librarian, Florence E. Sweeney, and pored over the records of the hospital.

Dr. Knowlton had been connected with the hospital only since 1939, Miss Sweeney since 1931. Neither of them nor anyone then connected with the hospital had any knowledge of events that had taken place in the hospital back in the nineteenth century. But the records were complete, going back to the opening of the hospital in 1832, and in filing cabinets, folders and large bound volumes there remained intact the records of patient admissions, births and adoptions.

The interest of the attorneys centered on the years 1887 and 1888 and particularly on births during the month of February of those years. The ancient bound volumes for each of the years, listing the names of patients by day and month, were procured from the archives. Then from the store-room, where they had been buried for over half a century, were recovered the individual case records of the patients who had given birth to children in the hospital during the months of February 1887 and 1888.

These individual case records were carefully scanned by the director, the librarian and the three lawyers. They were studied for the names of the mothers and fathers, the latter name frequently not being given in the case of unwed mothers, and for any showing of adoptions. There was an average of slightly over one birth a day, so more than sixty files were given close attention. It was when case number 6230 was reached that eyes lighted up and pulses beat faster for the intent attorneys.

Case number 6230 was Addie Weston, who, according to the record, entered the hospital at 10:30 in the evening of February 25, 1887, and at 10:10 in the morning of the twenty-sixth gave birth to a boy. The admission sheet stated that the patient was twenty-two years of age and unmarried. The place for the name of the father was blank.

The daily clinical record of the patient showed that on March 8 the baby was adopted. And appended to the file was a single piece of paper, a simple document. It was dated March 8, 1887. It was in two parts, an upper half and a lower half.

The upper recited, "I, Addie Weston, hereby consent to give my baby—a boy—to the within named for adoption." The lower read, "I, Mrs. Mary O'Donnell, hereby agree to take the within named baby—a boy—for adoption." The document was witnessed by "L. A. Cliff".

There was considerable discussion among the lawyers about the several handwritings appearing in the document. No one could say at the time who had written any part of the paper or even who had written the signatures "Addie Weston" and "Mrs.

I

Mary O'Donnell". This much was eventually agreed on and stipulated between the attorneys when the document was later placed before the court—that none of the writing and neither of the signatures was in the handwriting of Mabel Seymour Greer, and likewise that none of the writing and neither of the signatures was in the handwriting of Mary T. Segur, the former Mary Theresa O'Donnell.

Further examination of the hospital records established these additional relevant facts: that no other male child had been born in the hospital on February 26, 1887; that no child had been born on February 16 or February 26, 1888; and that the only male child born in the hospital in the months of February 1887 and 1888 who had been taken for adoption was the child of Addie Weston, born on February 26, 1887, and taken for adoption by Mary O'Donnell.

Friedman maintained a stiff upper lip throughout the examination of the documents and ensuing discussion. He refused to admit that the record of this birth referred to his client, since the signature of "Mrs. Mary O'Donnell" could not be identified with the Mary Theresa O'Donnell who had adopted Harold Segur. The similarity of names was such a coincidence, however, and the identification of Harold Segur in his later adoption papers as a child born in the Boston Lying-In Hospital on February 16, 1887, was so close to the child born in the hospital on February 26, 1887, that Friedman must have had faint hope in any argument that they were not the same and that Harold Segur was not the child of "Addie Weston".

The argument that appeared more promising and on which he seized with fervour was that no one knew who Addie Weston was and no one could say that the name was not a blind for Mabel Seymour. The Boston address given as Addie Weston's place of residence was meaningless, as no search there, sixty

Boston March 8th 1887.

I Addie Britton. hereby consent
to give my baby - a boy. to the within
named for adoption

Boston March 8th. 1887.

I Mrs Mary O'Donnell hereby agree
to take the within named baby - a boy.
for adoption

Witness to signature L. A. Cleff

Adoption paper from the Boston Lying-In Hospital

years afterward, would produce a thing. The fact that the signature of "Addie Weston" was not in the handwriting of Mrs. Greer lost any significance in view of the fact that the signature of "Mrs. Mary O'Donnell" was not in the handwriting of Mary Theresa O'Donnell.

One other witness was interviewed by the attorneys on that eventful day in Boston in June 1947. She was Dr. Frederica Cliff, the daughter of Dr. L. A. Cliff, who had died in 1929. Dr. Frederica Cliff practiced medicine in Boston from the same address from which her father had practised before her. She knew a great deal about his practise but nothing of an Addie Weston or a Mary Theresa O'Donnell. The one thing that she could say with certainty was that the signature "L. A. Cliff" on the document of adoption, dated March 8, 1887, was the true signature of her father.

Wells and Cox were elated with the Boston excursion. They were confident that they had documented Harold Segur's birth. The jigsaw puzzle had been pieced together to that extent. The pieces fitted—the adoption paper of 1887 and the adoption paper of 1901. There was a ragged edge in the absence of a genuine signature of Mary Theresa O'Donnell on the former, but still the pattern was perfect. Perfect—except for the missing piece. Who was Addie Weston?

In the days that followed, in the kind of thinking that lawyers do about their cases, the more Wells and Cox contemplated the showing of the hospital records the more concerned they became about the identity of Addie Weston; the more they realized that Segur had an escape from their net. If they remained unable to show that Addie Weston was a true name of a real person, other than Mrs. Greer, Friedman would always be able to contend that the birth record proved nothing as to Harold Segur's parentage. "Addie Weston" might well be a name which Mabel Seymour had assumed for the purpose of her confinement.

The more apparent it became, therefore, to the lawyers opposing Segur, that they would never be able to button up their case unless and until they could identify Addie Weston and show that the name was not just one taken by Mabel Seymour to disguise her identity. But how on earth could one go about finding a person who belonged to a name sixty years ago, with nothing more than the name to go on? How would one even begin such a search?

17

"Humpty Dumpty"

* * * * *

COURT proceedings, although not a show, are apt to bear some resemblance to the theatre. In fact, the two do have much in common.

What meets the eye in the finished production on the stage is only a synthesis and refinement of the work, thought and effort which have preceded. What goes on behind the scenes is responsible for what appears before the footlights. The imaginative conception, research, script writing, editing, casting, rehearsing and staging make the finished effects, and they constitute nine-tenths of the production, of which the public is hardly conscious.

The same is true of a court production. It goes off rather quickly, relatively smoothly and, if well done, with calculated effects. But the amount of work which has gone on before is apt to be prodigious, unseen and unappreciated. The trial lawyer, frequently to his chagrin, cannot create or choose his characters, write their lines or be sure of their performance. But he does have to find them, learn what they can say and give them a legitimate amount of direction and rehearsal before putting them on display. Furthermore, in a complicated case, he will have to engage in wide research for his material and probably will find that only a small part of it is usable. When he is finished with all this, he must put it together in an order and with a movement which will hold the interest and win the approval of the audience. There is no more critical audience than judge or jury.

The Greer case took, in all, ten days to try, although the trial was spread over several months. Before the case was ever moved into court, however, months of search went into gathering facts and collecting witnesses. One avenue led into another and down countless byways. Evidence on many points was elusive or impossible to obtain. Many lanes ended in dead ends. And even after the trial was well under way, adjournments were required to track down some document or witness which had become crucial because of what had appeared. For every day that the lawyers spent in court, therefore, presenting their finished case, many days were spent out of court garnering evidence.

The witnesses were mainly procured from Mrs. Greer's household and circle of friends and from a telephone listing she had made. Other witnesses had read about the case in the public Press and had offered information which led to other witnesses. They required checking and double checking. The search for documents was far and wide. Neither side was ever satisfied, and the course which led on and on seemed at times to be both never ending and leading nowhere.

Still, due to the assiduity of counsel, their devotion to their clients' interests, and their sense of responsibility to the court, an amazing amount of significant evidence and all available witnesses were collected. The completed showing left definite impressions, although all questions were not answered and much remained speculative or disputed.

There is, thus, another difference between a dramatic production and a court production. The playwright can order his ending. The judge or jury frequently have to determine the ending of the court case without all the information they would like and without knowing for certain whether they have reached the right result.

Cox and Wells had the advantage of numbers over Friedman and much greater financial resources for their production. Wells, as attorney for the estate, had its wealth to draw upon. Cox, as attorney for the Public Administrator, could count on the court's allowing him at least reimbursement of his expenses from the estate. So Wells and Cox had freedom of movement, which they required in their search and research, knowing that expenses necessarily incurred for the estate's protection and proper administration would be paid from the estate itself. Friedman, on the other hand, had neither help nor financial backing. He had only himself and hope. He was wise enough with that limitation not to attempt too much and to keep his case simple and to hammer away at the points in his favour, while Cox and Wells roamed farther afield in their search for evidence.

Hearings in the "Matter of Mabel Seymour Greer" were resumed in the Surrogate's Court on June 25, 1947. At ten o'clock in the morning once more the crier pronounced his chant, once more the Honourable James A. Delehanty ascended the bench, and counsel were in place at the counsel table.

It started as a prosaic morning, with Wells reading and marking into evidence the testimony and documents which had been taken at the Boston Lying-In Hospital. But as the documents, more eloquent than a dozen witnesses, loomed into meaning, it became an exciting morning. Here was the telltale trail. After the confusion and contradiction of the witnesses, the records seemed to provide clarity and certainty. As he followed closely each step in the documentary development, the wise judge said to himself, "Now we are beginning to get somewhere."

Aloud he asked, "What have you gentlemen learned about Addie Weston?"

"Nothing as yet, your Honour," Wells had to reply, "but we are diligently pursuing the matter."

"Nothing" echoed in Friedman's ears, and he hoped earnestly that there would continue to be nothing, unless by some unforeseen favourable turn of fortune it might affirmatively appear that "Addie Weston" was Mrs. Greer.

Although not prepared to enlighten the court with respect to the identity of Addie Weston, Wells was prepared to throw some further light on Mrs. Greer. During the weeks that the case had been in recess, letters and telephone calls had been received, as hoped for, from numerous individuals purporting to have information about the past life of Mrs. Greer. Even the judge had received communications, which he always turned over to the lawyers. Some of the information was bizarre and, if it contained any element of truth, it either could not be verified or was of no consequence to the issues in the case. There were the usual crank letters and anonymous calls which could be dismissed as worthless or which only led up blind alleys. But there were some worth-while communications from honestly helpful and responsible people. One was from the lady whom Wells called as his first witness—Mrs. Elise Hamilton Weisbecker of Southampton, Long Island.

The lady, though no longer young, had a lithe, compact figure. The shapely legs that showed below her skirt would still have passed the footlights test. Observing her on the witness stand, one would almost have expected her to whirl into a dance. Preliminary questioning brought out that she was a widow, that her maiden name was Hamilton and that she had been born in 1888.

Wells handed her the wedding photograph of Mrs. Greer and asked, "Have you ever seen the person whose picture appears in that photograph?"

"Yes, I have" came the prompt reply.

"When did you first see that person?"

"In 1904."

"What name, as you recall, did that person have or go under at that time?"

"Polly Ernest."

There was an audible intake of breath on the part of all the spectators, in which Friedman shared. The judge lifted his eyes, which had been at rest on the bench, and concentrated them on the witness.

"Where did you meet Polly Ernest in 1904?" Wells inquired.

"I met her in a play called *Humpty Dumpty*, played at the New Amsterdam Theater."

"What part did you have in that play called *Humpty Dumpty*?"

"I was a dancer."

"What relationship did Polly Ernest have to the play *Humpty Dumpty*?"

"She was a show girl."

"Will you tell me in more detail what you mean by the words 'show girl'?" Wells asked.

"Well, she didn't dance. She just wore pretty costumes."

"Is it correct for me to state that she was in the chorus?" the lawyer interpreted.

"She was in the chorus," the witness agreed.

The play remained five months in New York, Mrs. Weisbecker informed the court, then had a run in Boston, and during this time she and her sister, who was also in the play, were with Polly Ernest most of the time.

The friendship did not end with the end of *Humpty Dumpty*, and in time the sisters knew Mrs. Greer both as Mabel Seymour and as Mabel Greer. The last time the witness saw Mrs. Greer was in 1938. They had lunch together just before Mrs. Weisbecker moved to Southampton. After that Mrs. Greer called Mrs. Weisbecker several times by long distance, the last time only a month before Mrs. Greer died.

Against this background of familiarity with Mrs. Greer, Wells asked the witness the question which was his purpose in calling her: "What is your best opinion with regard to the age of Polly Ernest when you first met her in 1904?"

"Twenty-two or three" was her answer. "She was about my sister's age. I have often heard them talk about it."

"And how old was your sister?"

"She was born in 1882."

Mrs. Greer had never mentioned to Mrs. Weisbecker the birth of a child or the name Segur. Beyond saying that she was born in Manchester, England, Mrs. Greer had never said anything about her background or history before 1904.

"When you first met Polly back in 1904, was there anything which you observed with respect to her manner of speech?" Wells asked.

"Very soft and slow, very English," Mrs. Weisbecker assured him.

"Did she continue to have that accent through the years?"

"Yes, she did."

"That is all, thank you, Mrs. Weisbecker," Wells said politely, radiating his pleasure with her testimony.

Cox was satisfied and did not wish to inquire further. Friedman was far from satisfied but saw no purpose to be served by cross-examination, and he desisted. He knew that with Wells's care and thoroughness he would have amply checked on the production *Humpty Dumpty* and Mrs. Weisbecker's connection with the show. As to the age of Mrs. Greer, which was all that really mattered, he took the view that her testimony was only a matter of opinion and could count no more than the opinion of other witnesses who thought Mrs. Greer much older.

Friedman was quite justified in his confidence in Wells's care and in declining to challenge the identification made of Mrs. Greer by Mrs. Weisbecker, for Wells had tracked down other members of the cast of *Humpty Dumpty,* and the testimony of Mrs. Weisbecker was completely buttressed by the evidence given by the next witness. Mrs. Viola Henderson had been located in Atlantic City, where she operated a diaper service. Wells described her in a memorandum to Cox, after interviewing her, as a "well-preserved woman, endowed with an open and jolly nature". He said, "Mrs. Henderson will make an excellent witness. She is extremely clear and lucid."

Mrs. Henderson, as Viola Cecil, had played in *Humpty Dumpty* in 1904. She was a member of the chorus and one of the girls depicting "Black Coral of the Sea". They wore black tights covered with silver sequins and very large black hats. They made a striking picture, she recalled.

When Mrs. Henderson was shown the wedding picture of Mrs. Greer, she immediately identified her as the Polly Ernest of *Humpty Dumpty.*

She remembered Polly Ernest very well, and described her as plump, about five feet six inches in height, with very dark brown hair made up in pompadour style, creamy skin and a peach-bloom complexion. Polly had a rounded and somewhat upturned chin with a dimple in the upper lip. Her right eye had a tendency to squint. She spoke in a low and slow tone of voice and had a distinct English accent. "She had a little mannerism when she would be talking to you," the witness said. "She would sort of lean over and kind of squint one eye and speak in a rather confidential way, as if she were telling you something of great importance."

Mrs. Henderson was positive from the personal appearance of Polly at the time she first met her in 1904 that Polly was between twenty-two and twenty-four years of age. It was impossible that Polly could have been thirty at the time because, as Mrs. Henderson explained knowingly, Ned Wayburn and the others in charge of the chorus would have noted a girl of thirty and she would have had no chance for that type of show. A girl of thirty was limited to burlesque.

Mrs. Weisbecker and Mrs. Henderson were the first to draw the curtain aside and reveal something of the life of Mrs. Greer prior to 1908. They were also the curtain raisers in the courtroom battle over Mrs. Greer's age. That subject had been in the wings throughout the case and was now moving into the centre of the stage. Some of the witnesses who had previously appeared had incidentally touched on the question. But before the end of the case, witnesses in equal numbers and with equal qualifications to speak would be lined up in diametrically opposite positions and express opinions of Mrs. Greer's age that were ten years apart.

The question was bound to be a central issue in the case because, when all was said and done, however closely Harold Segur might match Mrs. Greer's description of her child, if Mrs. Greer had been born as late as 1880 she could not have been his mother. The ten-year spread in opinion as to her age was thus the measure of possibility of Harold Segur's being her son.

Wells knew how fallible judgments could be in estimating age. He was therefore anxious to rest his case in this particular on a stronger foundation than personal observations. With great care and diligence he had combed the city at every point of possible information to locate any records which might exist and bear on Mrs. Greer's age. He had been rewarded and took comfort in the fact that the records, so far as available, definitely supported his position. He lost no time in following up the dramatic introduction of the subject of age, made through Mrs. Greer's former companions on the stage, with the even more eloquent documents.

First, he placed in evidence the application for a licence to marry, signed by Louis Morris Greer and Mabel Adele Seymour on November 19, 1908. This was the document in which Mabel Seymour had stated that her age was twenty-seven and that she had been born in Manchester, England, the daughter of James Seymour and Charlotte Barnes.

This was followed by the marriage certificate, which also gave Mrs. Greer's age as twenty-seven, although giving a birth date of January 28, 1884.

Next Wells offered the record of the United States Census of 1920, showing Mrs. Greer's age in that year as thirty-nine and stating that she had been born in England and had emigrated to the United States in 1900.

A voting register of October 8, 1920, recorded her age as thirty-eight and the fact that she had been a resident of this country for twenty years.

Three savings-account records were placed in evidence. In opening one account in 1932, Mrs. Greer had stated her year of birth as 1881. In another, opened the same year, she had stated her age as forty-eight, thus placing her birth date in 1884. And in an account opened in 1935, she had stated that she was born on January 28, 1882.

Finally, Wells produced the admission charts of the New York Eye and Ear Infirmary, where Mrs. Greer had twice been a patient. On her first admission, in the year 1943, she had given her date of birth as January 28, 1881, her age as 62, her birthplace England. On her second admission in 1946, she had merely stated her age as over twenty-one and her birthplace as Scotland.

Thus, as far as the documents showed, whenever Mrs. Greer stated the day of her birth she consistently said January 28, although the year varied from 1881 to 1884. In any event, if these documents were to be accepted, she could not have been the mother of Harold Segur.

Friedman had no documents to contradict this showing and had to content himself for the moment with the observation that Mrs. Greer had been very free with the selection of the year of her birth, as with the place, and that she had undoubtedly indulged in a lady's privilege of making out that she was much younger than she actually was.

18

A Wild-Goose Chase

*   *   *   *   *

THE case against Segur was beginning to take shape like a military campaign on a battle map. There were three prongs of attack or objectives. One was to show that Segur had been born in the Boston Lying-In Hospital, the child of Addie Weston. A second was to produce strong, if not conclusive, evidence that Mrs. Greer had been of an age that would make it impossible for her to have been the mother of Harold Segur. The third, and by far the most difficult, was to show who Addie Weston was and thus affirmatively establish Segur's parentage and eliminate Mrs. Greer as his mother beyond question.

With the records of the Lying-In Hospital, Wells and Cox were satisfied as to the first objective. It remained for them only to call Mr. Henry Wise, who had been the attorney for Harold Segur as administrator of Mary Segur's estate, to reinforce their position. They also had a number of persons, besides those already called, who would testify to Mrs. Greer's appearing to be the age the records indicated she was. As to the identity of Addie Weston, however, they didn't have a clue.

While the hearings were in recess and while the hearings were going on, Wells and Cox spent many hours in discussing how they might trace Addie Weston. Nothing in the hospital records, other than a long outdated residence, indicated anything as to her whereabouts, and no other record which had turned up as much as mentioned her. No witness, with the exception of Mr. Wise, who was to be called, had ever heard of Addie Weston, and Wise knew of her only as a name appearing in the hospital records.

Was she still alive? Had she married or changed her name? Where in the world might she have moved? Had there ever been such a person as Addie Weston? No one had the slightest idea. To try to find her was worse than looking for a needle in a haystack, because not even the location of the haystack was known.

The task became none the easier for thought. Thought did produce, however, the only possibility of locating Addie Weston, dead or alive, although the process would be painful and was not promising. On the assumption, which was at least probable, that Addie Weston was a resident of Massachusetts, it occurred to Wells and Cox that she might by chance be located through the office of one of the registries of deeds or wills of the counties in the state of Massachusetts. In each county a record is kept of conveyances and wills. The indexes in these county offices would reveal the names of persons disposing of property by will or deed. Undoubtedly the name of Weston would appear many times over, down the years, in all the places where such records are kept. If, wherever it appeared back in the ancient records, the file were examined, the name of Addie Weston might appear, as one mentioned, for example, in a will of her father.

The undertaking of such research in every county of Massachusetts was something to contemplate. "It would be a wild-goose chase," commented Wells. "Sure," admitted Cox, "but that is the way you catch a wild goose."

So, while they proceeded with the presentation of the evidence they had in hand, their minions were set at the task of going from county seat to county seat in the Commonwealth of Massachusetts to see what the records relating to anyone by the name of Weston might disclose. They started with Boston and after several days drew a blank. The order of procedure then decided on was to take the counties adjoining Boston and move outward as far as necessary or until every county in the state had been covered. Aside from the doubt that the extensive and expensive search would produce anything, there was the question of whether the job could be done within the time the court might allow.

Meanwhile the case went on.

19

Henry Wise—Lawyer on the Trail

* * * * *

HENRY WISE, the Boston lawyer, was the only living link with sources of information of Harold Segur's parentage. All he knew was hearsay, but he at least had been on the trail when the tracks were fresher. He was a methodical person who had catalogued his information well and was a clear reporter of what he learned.

Under examination by Wells, he told the court that shortly after he was retained by Harold Segur in connection with his foster-mother's estate, Segur brought up the question of his paternity. Segur said that for all his life he had been very much concerned to determine who his father and mother were, that he would give anything to find out, and asked the lawyer to help him.

"Did he give you anything to go on?" Wells asked.

"He said," the lawyer reported, "that he recalled as a young boy the name 'Baker' as a name of a man who had been in touch with Mrs. Segur, and as one of the avenues or alternatives for search he asked me to find out whether possibly he may have been the son of this man Baker. He also had in the back of his mind that New York City might be the place of birth, so we correlated those two ideas, and in ordinary course I sent correspondence to the officials of the city here, but none of the reports received in reply indicated any record of a birth of one Harold A. Baker, so we stopped at that."

"Did Mary Theresa Segur ever tell you, and did you make any statements to Harold Segur, regarding her life prior to her marriage to Dr. Segur?"

"I think nothing other than that her maiden name was O'Donnell and she claimed that she was the wife of Baker."

"Now, Mr. Wise," Wells continued, "in connection with your efforts to obtain information for Harold Segur, did you communicate with the Boston Lying-In Hospital?"

"I did," the witness acknowledged.

"From what source did you ascertain that the Boston Lying-In Hospital was a possible place of inquiry?"

"Mrs. Segur had told me that she had acquired a child from the Boston Lying-In."

"After you received information from the Boston Lying-In Hospital, what did you do thereafter with respect to Harold A. Segur?"

"I wrote him this letter."

The witness handed over a copy of a letter dated February 8, 1928. This was the letter concerning which Wells had cross-examined Segur at length and about which Segur had been so vague. Wells marked it in evidence and handed it over to the judge. His "uhm" was inaudible as he read:

February 8, 1928

Mr. Harold A. Segur,
27 Foster Street,
Worcester, Mass.

Dear Sir:

Below is a copy of a record in the Boston Lying-In Hospital

relative to Addie Weston, age 22, of 79 Brighton Street, Boston, who gave birth to a male child February 26, 1887. I have paid the girl who dug up this record five dollars, and at your convenience you may send me a check covering this matter.

Boston, Mar. 8, 1887

I Addie Weston—hereby consent to give my baby—a boy —to the within named for adoption—

Boston, March 8, 1887

I, Mrs. Mary O'Donnell, hereby agree to take the within named baby—a boy—for adoption.

Witness to Signature—L. A. Cliff

Yours very truly,

Wells did not resume his questioning until the judge had laid the letter down. Then he asked, "Did you thereafter discuss with Harold Segur this record which you had obtained from the Lying-In Hospital?"

"Yes," the witness advised.

"What was the conversation?"

"I told him I had received a record from the Boston Lying-In, and that it led nowhere, as far as my ability to be helpful to determine his paternity."

Wells acknowledged to himself that the lawyer was strictly correct in stating that the record indicated nothing as to Harold Segur's paternity. It indicated a great deal, however, as to the identity of his mother—provided Addie Weston could be identified. There was that problem again, the loose end in the case. Would they ever be able to tie it up?

Coming out of his reverie, Wells asked, "Did Mr. Segur make any comment to you in reply to that statement?"

"He said—he sort of shrugged his shoulders—" and the witness shrugged his in imitation— "as if to say, 'Another dead-end road.'"

"Dead-end, yes," Wells reflected, unless those young men traversing the Massachusetts countryside in search of a trace of Addie Weston were favoured by fortune and found their mark.

But the witness had something more of significance to contribute.

"Did you make any inquiry concerning the L. A. Cliff whose signature appears at the bottom of the record?" Wells inquired.

"Yes," the witness replied.

"What was the nature of that inquiry?"

"I knew him. He had been my family doctor."

Fate, who is fickle in lawsuits as in life, had made one of those favourable interventions. She might have sealed off the approach to Addie Weston, but by another turn she had led Segur into the hands of a lawyer who personally knew Dr. Cliff, and Dr. Cliff was certainly a key to the riddle.

What Dr. Cliff knew had not died with him twenty years before his knowledge became important. It had been recorded in a memorandum which lawyer Wise had made of a conversation he had with Dr. Cliff in the doctor's office at 3:30 in the afternoon of January 14, 1928. In the circumstances, the lawyer was allowed to testify to the contents of his memorandum.

This was Dr. Cliff's story as recorded in Mr. Wise's notes: Mary Theresa O'Donnell kept house for Baker in Boston. He was a construction engineer and was required to go to Mexico to work on a railroad. She left with him and when they got as far as Atlanta a doctor there told her that she was pregnant and that it was not safe for her to go to Mexico. She returned to Boston and evidently had a miscarriage. One day she called Dr. Cliff and said, "I want to adopt a baby for certain reasons. Do you know a baby two or three weeks old?" The doctor said,

"Only place is at McLean Street, Lying-In." She hired a woman
to go down and get a boy baby. The woman went the next day
and brought back a three-week-old baby, light-blue eyes, "near-
est thing to Baker you could imagine." Shortly afterward Baker
returned and Dr. Cliff was called in. When he came to the
house Baker was walking up and down with the child and said,
"These women do not know how to take care of a baby. It takes
a man." The doctor was about to tell him how the baby got
there when Mary Theresa walked in and got Baker to go downstairs. She took the baby and said to the doctor, "He thinks
this is my baby."

Here, then, was the explanation of why the name "Mrs.
Mary O'Donnell" in the 1887 adoption record of the Lying-In
Hospital was not in the handwriting of Mary Theresa O'Donnell. Apparently she had sent someone else to the hospital to
get the baby, and such loose practice was allowed in those days.

After the reading of his memorandum, Mr. Wise resumed
his own testimony. He said that Mrs. Segur had told him that
she had obtained the child at the Lying-In Hospital with Dr.
Cliff's assistance and, therefore, he interviewed Dr. Cliff after
Harold Segur had asked him for help, but he never reported to
Segur what Dr. Cliff had told him.

"What else did you do and who else did you see, in addition
to this Dr. Cliff, with regard to the determination of the parents of Harold Segur?" Wells asked.

"No one," the witness advised, "other than Dr. Willard
Segur, from whom I tried to get some assistance."

The movement of the judge's head was almost impercepti-
ble. But his sense of the significant had been touched, and the
quickening interest with which he had listened to the testimony of the lawyer Wise reached intensity with Wells's following question.

"Will you tell us, Mr. Wise, in detail of your attempts in that regard and the results of those attempts?"

"I asked Harold Segur," the lawyer replied, "whether Dr. Segur might not be helpful, and I urged him to put queries to Dr. Willard Segur, which he said he did, and he got nothing which would be helpful. He then asked me to write or otherwise communicate with Dr. Segur, and I did. I wrote several letters, and one day Dr. Segur came to see me. I told him that Harold Segur had asked me to try to find out who his parents were and that Harold had said to me that he thought that he, Dr. Segur, could be helpful, and, as I recall it, I said it two or three times in two or three forms, and he was noncommunicative. He wouldn't answer."

"Did he make any answer to your statements?"

"Then, finally, before he departed—as a matter of fact, he never sat down—before he departed, in a rather angry tone, he said, 'I can't help you,' and he walked out."

"Were those the only statements made to you on that occasion?"

"That is all. He was very taciturn."

Dead quiet pervaded the courtroom as the witness finished his last answer and ushered out the day.

20

Frank Reitman—Meeting at Piping Rock

* * * * *

FRANK REITMAN, who had been chauffeur for the Greers
from 1930 to 1942, presented Wells with something of a
problem. Ordinarily when a lawyer produces a witness he
wants the court to believe his testimony and vouches for his
credibility. But Wells had no such attitude toward Reitman or
his story.

In the first place, Wells had no interest, even though it aided
in eliminating Harold Segur as the heir, in making it appear
that a possible genuine heir was hovering around. In the second
place, Wells shared the doubt which his associate Armbruster
had already cast on the Reitman story.

But Reitman and the Piping Rock incident had entered into
the evidence given by several of the witnesses, and it was important to know whether such an appearance of a person purporting to be Mrs. Greer's son, as they had told about, had
actually taken place. It would also be important to know
whether Segur was the person so appearing, although Segur
had denied any such part and his lawyer had already indicated

that he regarded the alleged Piping Rock appearance as sheer fabrication. And there was one other respect in which Reitman's testimony would be important. According to what he would say Mrs. Greer told him, about the date of birth and age of her son, Harold Segur was far from a possibility. So Wells felt that he was under a duty to call Reitman as a witness and give the court the opportunity of seeing and hearing him.

In substance Reitman told the story which was already familiar to the court about the Piping Rock incident. He placed it in August 1941 and stated that when he reported to Mrs. Greer the appearance of the man who claimed to be her son she broke down and told him the story of her child.

According to the witness, Mrs. Greer said that she had the child "somewhere around 1901 or 1902" when she was eighteen or nineteen years old; that Dr. Segur stopped paying the boarding house keeper after two and a half years, and then Mrs. Greer left the child because she had no money. Reitman quoted her as saying that she had "always been nervous for fear the son may pop up and Mr. Greer may find out about it", and that is why she had been a nervous woman. In an aside he added, "She was a very peculiar woman, you know."

"Did you describe the gentleman to Mrs. Greer?" Wells asked.

"I did," the witness replied. "She asked me how old do I think that boy was. I said, 'Well, somewheres around forty-four or forty-five or something like that,' and she says, 'No, he couldn't be that old. He should be about forty-one or forty-two.' I says, 'Well, now, Mrs. Greer, I am no judge of ages. I don't know.'"

"Did you tell Mrs. Greer anything else about the description of the gentleman that you had met?"

"She asked me about how he looked and all that. I says,

[141]

'Well,' I said, 'he was about five-ten and he weighed about 150 or 155 pounds, somewheres around there,' and she asked me, 'Was he a nice-looking chap?' and I said, 'Yes.' Then she asked me what kind of hair he had and what kind of eyes, and I told her that he had brown hair and I think grey—I think—I don't remember about the eyes, whether they were grey or blue."

Wells handed the witness a photograph which was agreed by counsel to be a fair representation of Harold Segur and said, "Mr. Reitman, I ask if you can identify the person of that photograph?"

"No, sir, that is not the gentleman," came the quick response.

"I ask you particularly," the lawyer pursued, "is that the gentleman with whom you had a conversation at the Piping Rock Country Club?"

"No, sir, that isn't the gentleman at all that I saw down at the Piping Rock Club," Reitman answered decisively.

On cross-examination, Friedman went after the witness with vigour. He pulled no punches in suggesting that Reitman had repeatedly conjured up the appearance of this pretended son for Mrs. Greer and had received payments from both Mr. and Mrs. Greer which were extraordinary.

"This man whom you saw, regarding whom you told Mrs. Greer, how many times did you see him?" Friedman asked exactingly.

"Oh, I saw him at least about four or five times," the witness replied.

The lawyer demanded that he detail the times and places. The witness responded that the meetings were over a period of about a year and aside from the first meeting were always in the vicinity of Park Avenue and Fifty-fourth Street, where the Greers lived.

"Did you tell Mrs. Greer every time you saw him that you had seen him?"

"Yes, sir, I did."

"How much salary were you receiving for your employment with Mrs. Greer?" was the next question.

"Five dollars a day" was the answer.

Prepared with cancelled cheques to back up his further questioning of the witness on the subject of other payments made to him by Mr. and Mrs. Greer, Friedman brought out that Reitman had received $250 from Mrs. Greer in August 1942, which he explained as being for some operation. From September 1942 to the end of the year, while unemployed, he received $150 a month from Mr. Greer. Then he went to work for the Air Force until June 1943, and in August 1943 Mr. Greer bought him a taxi which he thereafter used as a taxi operator.

With this showing, Friedman dismissed the witness.

21

Tom Touhy—A Coachman
Looks Back

* * * * *

BEFORE Frank Reitman chauffeured for the Greers, Tom
Touhy had served in that capacity for the fourteen years
between 1910 and 1924. Indeed before that, as a carriage
driver, he had occasionally driven for Mrs. Greer.

"When did you first meet Mrs. Greer?" Wells asked him.

Beetle brows drew together, taxing memory for an exactness
befitting the importance of the occasion. Then the man replied, slowly, carefully and extensively, "Well, when I first met
Mrs. Greer it was about thirty-seven years ago—thirty-eight—
I ain't sure which, but around that time, but at that time I had
only driven her a few times from a renting stable—horses. That
is the. Knickerbocker Stable in Fifty-fourth Street, right off
Broadway, but it was only occasionally I——"

Wells interrupted the flow. "If you will just wait, Mr.
Touhy, I will ask you the questions, and we will develop what
is relevant. You say you met Mrs. Greer about thirty-eight
years ago. What was the occasion of your first meeting Mrs.
Greer?"

"Well, she hired this carriage, private carriage."

"Was Mrs. Greer known as Mrs. Greer at the time you first met her?"

"No, her name was Mabel Seymour."

"Can you recall where Mable Seymour was then living?"

"Seymour Hotel, Forty-fifth Street, right off Fifth Avenue, between Fifth and Sixth."

To the point, Wells inquired, "How old did Mabel Seymour impress you as being at the time that you first met her?"

"Well," the witness replied with continuing care, "I figured she was at that time a very young-looking girl, it seems to me around twenty-six, maybe twenty-seven, around that, but I don't think she was any more than that, as far as I can see. Of course, I am only giving my estimation."

Wells skipped over the years and asked, "When was the last time you saw Mrs. Greer?"

"Well, I came up from the country to see her, just before her death."

"What age, in your opinion, was Mrs. Greer when you last saw her?"

"Well, she was just as fresh and as strong as ever," Mr. Touhy opined. "I was very much surprised she went off so quick."

The judge gently broke in. "The question is how old you thought she was."

"I wouldn't say she was more than sixty-five" was the final response.

22

Olin Chester Potter—Proprietor
of the Inn

*   *   *   *   *

IF TODAY one travels from New York to the Berkshires
along that verdant valley between the Hudson and the
Housatonic known as the Harlem Valley, he will be beckoned
off the concrete highway by an arresting sign, pointing the way
down a dirt road to the Old Drovers Inn.

Long before the highway was there the road ambled across
the countryside, trod by drovers driving their pigs and sheep
to the market at Dover. The rambling white house that even
then proclaimed itself as an inn had settled into the slope of
the land so that the traveller could enter below into the tavern
or above into lodgings. The upstairs rooms were a crazy quilt of
sizes and shapes. But the downstairs was a large single room
with a huge stone fireplace in the centre, opening on two sides,
in which a whole sheep or pig could be roasted, and around
which a goodly company could gather for food, drink or talk.
The thick foundation walls were insulation from the wintry
blasts, and the fire and drink were warming to the outer and

inner man. By summer the same thick walls and cooling drink provided relief from the dusty road and heat.

The old drover has long since disappeared from the land-scape, but the inn, much the same, still stands and is as inviting to any modern traveller speeding over the rolling hills as it was to those foot travellers of another age, or as it was to Mr. and Mrs. Louis Morris Greer on their frequent visits to the Berk-shires. The upper rooms are elegant now with period pieces and chintz. The stone of the tavern walls, the floor and the fire-place are just the same. The fire burns more gently, the con-versation is more polite and the laughter perhaps less hearty. But nothing could be more cheering or refreshing than to spend a luncheon or dinner hour in this setting and partake of the excellent fare of table and cellar.

The host for many years, Olin Chester Potter, was an urbane gentleman and fine restaurateur. The inn, under his proprie-torship, was the rural counterpart of his excellent restaurant in the city. The Greers delighted in Olin Chester Potter and his restaurants. They expressed their appreciation not only in their patronage but in the gift of some of the fine furniture which adorns the upstairs rooms of the Old Drovers. Their re-gard for him was deep in the years. For on that day in 1924, when Mr. Potter opened his first restaurant in New York, near the Greer residence, they came for dinner. They dined there most of the nights they were in the city for the next many years.

Mr. Potter was not accustomed to going to court, but he was perfectly at ease in the witness chair.

"When did you first meet Mabel Seymour Greer?" Wells asked.

"On the sixteenth day of October 1924" was the definite answer.

The lawyer took note and commented, "I notice that you refer to October 16, 1924, as a particular date. Can you tell me why you do so?"

"Yes, it was the opening of the first restaurant that I had in New York City, and Mrs. Greer was our first paying customer. She bought and paid for the first luncheon that we served."

"Did you see both Mrs. Greer and Mr. Greer thereafter?"

"Yes, I saw them both that night for dinner, and for the next twelve years at 121 East Fifty-second Street we saw them as often as six nights a week."

Mr. Potter told of his friendship with the Greers, his visits to their home in New York City and on Long Island, and of seeing them in England and Scotland. He had certainly had ample opportunity to observe Mrs. Greer and form an opinion of her age.

"Can you tell me what, in your opinion, was Mrs. Greer's age at the time you first met her in 1924?" Wells asked.

"I would say she was a woman somewhere between forty-two and forty-five years old," the witness answered without hesitation.

"When did you last see Mabel Seymour Greer?"

"I saw her in June 1946. I had tea with her."

"What, in your opinion, was Mrs. Greer's age when you last saw her?"

"I should say she was about sixty-five, not more."

"In your conversations with Mrs. Greer, did you observe anything with respect to her speech or mode of speech?" Wells inquired.

Yes, Mr. Potter did. "She had a faltering mode of speech. She spoke very slowly and very distinctly."

"Did she have what you might characterize as an accent?"

"Yes. A Yorkshire accent."

"You may examine," said Wells to Friedman, the invitation scarcely concealing a challenge.

Friedman was not to be ensnared into one of those cross-examinations which draws only the emphasis of repetition for the pains of questioning. He had a stratagem for a single question, but it didn't work.

"Mrs. Greer was a woman who took care of herself very well?" he asked suggestively.

"I don't think she took care of herself very well" was the negative reply.

"She did not?" Friedman said with apparent surprise.

"I don't think she did, no," the witness retorted. "She wasn't a woman who spent a great deal of time at the beauty parlours or went to reducing exercises or anything of that sort."

"Do you know what Mrs. Greer did in her off time?" the lawyer asked testingly.

"I don't know exactly, no," Mr. Potter conceded. But in reaffirmation of his long acquaintance with her, he added, "I just know we saw a great deal of her."

23

Adjournment

* * * * *

WELLS had almost reached the end of his evidence. In fact, he had only one more witness to call—unless in quick order the unexpected happened and someone was found who could answer the question, Who was Addie Weston? Two young lawyers, the agents of Wells and Cox, had been scouring the Massachusetts countryside for weeks now, delving into musty records of long-forgotten transactions, and they had found nothing touching on an Addie Weston. She might as well never have existed. Perhaps she never did exist and was just a name assumed by someone to bring an illegitimate child into the world, thus closing the door on the late pursuers but leaving it open for Friedman to maintain that, like "Polly Ernest," "Addie Weston" was just another name for Mabel Seymour Greer.

The time had come, therefore, to disclose to the court the efforts they were making to locate Addie Weston and to ask for more time in which to carry on their search. This would be the second request for an adjournment and, although they hoped it would be granted, Wells and Cox had no doubt that they were approaching the end of the court's indulgence and the end of time and chance to prove the reality of the person whose name had come to haunt them.

In the absence of evidence as to the identity of Addie Weston, the lawyers opposing Segur were putting more and more emphasis on the matter of Mrs. Greer's age and driving home the point, they hoped, that she could not have been Harold Segur's mother. The last day of the trial had been occupied with this evidence, and they chose to close the point, and perhaps the entire case, with the receptionist for the photographer who had taken Mrs. Greer's wedding picture—the picture which had been used for identification purposes throughout the trial.

There was another touch of fate, Wells thought as he presented her testimony, in the availability of Mrs. Gertrude Winburn as a witness. Mrs. Winburn had not only received Mrs. Greer at the Aimee Dupont Studio that day in 1908 when Mrs. Greer came to have her picture taken, but of recent years she had lived in the same apartment house as Mrs. Greer and knew her personally. And having been associated with the business of photography most of her life, being the wife of and receptionist for Jay Te Winburn, one of New York's leading photographers, Mrs. Winburn should be accepted as a good observer and judge of age.

Mrs. Winburn testified that she first saw Mrs. Greer on the occasion of the taking of the wedding picture and last saw her two weeks before she died. She was thus prepared to express an opinion of Mrs. Greer's age both at the time of her marriage and at the time of her death. Mrs. Winburn's opinion was that Mrs. Greer had been twenty-eight when she had the picture taken in 1908, and sixty-six when she died in 1946. In fact, Mrs.

Winburn stated, only shortly before Mrs. Greer died she told Mrs. Winburn that she was sixty-six.

With the conclusion of this testimony, Wells asked for a conference of counsel with the judge. The court rose and the three lawyers followed the man who was presiding over the destiny of their case into his chambers, a large room of the period of the courtroom, half office with wide desk and straight chairs, half lounge with sofa and easy chairs. The separation between the two was as definite as the division between the judge's official and social personality.

Not exactly genial at any time, the judge was nevertheless gracious and friendly in social intercourse and enjoyed relaxing with friends and visitors and always made them comfortable in that part of his chambers set apart for the purpose. In conference on judicial business, however, he was always businesslike and never let his callers forget their mission or the value of time. On this occasion he took his seat at his desk and motioned counsel to the straight chairs. With the single word "Yes?" he invited them to state their business.

Wells explained the venture he and Cox were engaged on in an endeavour to learn something about Addie Weston and said that time was needed to complete the investigation.

"How much time?" the judge asked.

"We don't know," said Wells, "but we have been at it since we discovered the birth record involving Addie Weston. We are making progress, although nothing of value has been uncovered yet. We recognize that we cannot put off the termination of this case indefinitely, but if your Honour will grant a month's adjournment now, we will undertake to finish our search in that time and then be prepared to offer something definite as to the identity of Addie Weston or confess that we can find nothing more."

"Do you have anything further, Mr. Friedman?" the judge inquired of counsel for Segur.

Friedman said that he had some witnesses ready on the subject of Mrs. Greer's age.

"Very well," concluded the judge. "We will take up your witnesses tomorrow, Mr. Friedman. Then we will adjourn to August 11, at which time the case must finish."

The conference was ended. The lawyers filed out, and the judge settled down to a consideration of other matters far removed from the Greer case.

24

A Matter of Age

* * * * *

FRIEDMAN was unable to understand the discrepancy in opinion as to Mrs. Greer's age among those who had known her. He did not question the honesty of any of the witnesses who had been called by the other side. Yet he believed that they were in error, and he had taken pains to find other persons, qualified to speak by reason of their contacts with Mrs. Greer, who would support his own version of her age. He now had a number of such witnesses and would have to place great reliance on them, for unless he could show that it was possible for Mrs. Greer to have borne a child in 1887 or 1888, the case would go against him regardless of other considerations.

The first witness he called was Mrs. Dessie Morris Delgado, a first cousin of Mr. Greer, who had known Mrs. Greer all her married life. It was no pleasure for this gentle lady, member of a family which had always had a distaste for publicity, to occupy the witness chair and tell of a long intimacy with the woman who in death had given the family a notoriety long avoided. But caught in the net of this case, she did not wince and answered with scrupulous frankness the questions put to her.

"When did you first meet Mrs. Greer?" Friedman asked.

"I met Mrs. Greer in 1908."

"Mrs. Delgado, in your opinion, what was the age of Mrs. Greer when you first met her in 1908?"

"Approximately, I should say, between thirty-five and thirty-eight. She was not in her earliest youth."

"Subsequent to 1908 you came to live in New York?"

"Yes, I came to live in New York in 1912."

"From 1912 on, did you see Mr. and Mrs. Greer frequently?"

"I had dinner on the average of three and four times a week with them. I saw her constantly."

"During the time that you saw Mrs. Greer, did you ever have any conversation with her with respect to places where she desired to go?"

What is this? thought Wells and Cox simultaneously, sensitive to the sudden shift in the course of the questioning. The examination of Mrs. Delgado until this moment had been in the groove, following an anticipated course, and there had been nothing to cause Wells or Cox to regard her as more than an ordinary witness who would testify unfavourably to them on the question of age. But with the last question they pricked up their ears and sensed danger. In the next instant, the bomb fell.

"Yes," reflected the witness. "Mrs. Greer kept at me constantly for three years to please take her to Worcester, Massachusetts."

"Which three years were they?"

"Well, the last three years that she lived."

"In the course of these conversations did you ask her why she was desirous of going to Worcester?"

"Yes. I asked her why she always kept at me to go to Worcester, and her answer was 'And wouldn't you be surprised.' "

With this détour from the question of age, neatly executed and evening an old score with Wells and Cox on account of their early efforts with Annie Jackson to make it appear that Mrs. Greer had not known where her son could be found, Friedman resumed the road, slightly smug from the sensation he had created.

"When did you last see Mrs. Greer alive?" he asked.

"I saw Mrs. Greer in March of 1945. That is the last time that I saw her," Mrs. Delgado replied.

"In your opinion, what was her age at that time?"

"Well, I should have said that Mrs. Greer was certainly seventy-four years old then."

"During the lifetime of Mr. Greer, did he ever speak to you with respect to the age of his wife?"

Back on the road, yes, but Wells and Cox felt another bump coming. Cox instinctively rose to it. "Your Honour, I object, not binding on the estate."

Wells interjected, "I object also."

"Overruled," said the judge.

The witness answered, "He told me that she was six years older than I."

"When were you born, Mrs. Delgado?" Friedman inquired.

"Eighteen eighty-one."

"In your opinion, she was more than six years older than you are?" the lawyer asked as a calculation from her previous testimony.

This drew an objection which was sustained. "The witness has told us her opinion of Mrs. Greer's age," the judge observed. "You do the arithmetic."

There was little to be accomplished by cross-examination, Wells and Cox agreed. Perhaps the less the better. One line of questioning might be worth a try—suggesting that the family of Mr. Greer did not approve of his marriage and that the witness as a member of the family was prejudiced against Mrs. Greer. The insinuation took only to the extent of bringing out that Mr. Greer's sister was "not very happy" over the marriage.

"And you and your mother joined in the sister's views in that regard, did you not?" Wells suggested.

"No," replied the witness. "We didn't know Mabel and had no reason to object."

Saleswomen are good judges of age. They are accustomed to looking observantly at people. The vision of Virginia Morris was now dim with her seventy-eight years, but her eyes had been keen when she worked at Altman's in the '20s and her memory was still clear. Mrs. Greer had been in the habit of shopping at Altman's and had formed quite an attachment for Miss Morris. She had frequently asked Miss Morris to come to her apartment to consult with her.

As a witness called by Friedman, Miss Morris was "sure" that Mrs. Greer had been around fifty when she first met her in 1920 and that she had been over seventy when they last met in 1941.

Nurses are perhaps even better judges of age. The physiological is their business. Yvonne Paradis was a registered nurse. She had taken care of Mr. Greer when he was a patient in the Doctors Hospital for two months in the spring of 1938. And in 1946, shortly before Mrs. Greer's death, she had rendered some professional service to her. Miss Paradis had seen Mrs. Greer every day during Mr. Greer's hospitalization in 1938, and had seen her several times in 1940 or 1941, as well as during her last illness in 1946.

Miss Paradis testified that in 1938 Mrs. Greer had told her that she had a son fifty years old, and in 1946, in a conversation respecting age, when Miss Paradis expressed the opinion that Mrs. Greer looked older than she purported to be, Mrs. Greer stated that she had "changed her age before she married Mr. Greer".

Both sides had had their innings on the issue of age. It would seem that the witnesses on the two sides were not talking about the same person. A full ten years' difference in opinion existed between them. And the difference existed all along the line of Mrs. Greer's life, from her marriage to her death.

The difference could not be accounted for on the basis of varying opportunities of the witnesses to observe their subject. All had had virtually the same opportunities over a period of years. On what basis, then, could the difference be explained and the issue be resolved?

It would have been interesting to test judgments by having each witness express a present opinion as to the age of some person produced in court as a "guinea pig" for the purpose. This was not done, however, and the problem was left with the judge with no objective standard of judgment—only his own observation of the witnesses and his evaluation of the reliability of their observations.

Wells and Cox put their faith mainly in the records. They felt also that they had sufficiently fortified the records with other evidence to require the court to accept the records. Friedman earnestly argued, on the other hand, that the records, starting with Mrs. Greer's application for a marriage licence, were only her own word and represented an attempt, as she admitted to Miss Paradis, to change her age. She also had told Miss Paradis in 1938 that she had a son fifty years old, and that would exactly fit Harold Segur, born in 1888 or even 1887. Friedman hoped, therefore, that the judge would disregard the records and be persuaded that Mrs. Greer not only could have been but actually was Harold Segur's mother.

With this division of opinion and hope among the lawyers, the court adjourned for the period allowed Wells and Cox to exhaust the possibilities of finding Addie Weston.

25

Open Sesame!

* * * * *

ESSEX, Middlesex, Suffolk, Norfolk, Bristol, Plymouth are
the good English names of the counties of Massachusetts
that ring Boston. They are large and populous areas. Weston is
not an uncommon name in Massachusetts. Hundreds of Westons
have lived and died there these many years and recorded their
dispositions of property in the county offices. Looking through
the wills and deeds made by people with the name of Weston
over the last half century is thus a prodigious task.

It was a constant and unrewarding chore for two young
lawyers, frustrating in its prospects—going into office after
office, taking down the heavy, clothbound indexes, making a
listing of every Weston that appeared and noting the record
number of every document in the buried files in which a Weston
acted, descending into dark vaults and digging out the dusty
files, and reading, reading, reading the endless legal language
in which the wills and deeds were couched, fighting fatigue and
boredom in the labour of making sure that every mention of a
name is spotted and guarding against the risk that in a moment

of relaxation Addie, if perchance there, might still slip away.

The lawyers had been at this task for a month when the last adjournment of the Greer case was taken on June 30. They had completed the search in Essex, Middlesex, Suffolk and Norfolk and were deep in the records of Bristol at that time. They had been through reams and reams of legal papers and had made a catalogue of Westons—but no Addie.

By the end of the first week in July, the searchers had finished Bristol. They had added to the catalogue—but still no Addie.

In Plymouth there were records of Westons so numerous that the searchers feared they would not have time to go farther afield, and they hoped with a hope born of near exhaustion that here, if ever, Addie would be found.

It was on the thirteenth of July 1947 that the young men read the will of one William E. Weston of Duxbury, who had died in 1905 and remembered all his children, George, Maria, Etta, Eunice—and Addie.

"Open sesame!" shrieked one of the examiners.

"Eureka!" shouted the other.

The dust literally flew from the files of papers left behind as they rushed off to Duxbury, hot on the trail of Addie, hoping to find some Weston there who knew or remembered Addie, and perchance to find Addie herself.

Finding an Addie Weston meant only that there really was an Addie Weston, but whether she was the woman who sixty years before had borne a child in the Boston Lying-In Hospital was the question, and a wide gulf still separated the pursuers from the answer.

There was one member of the Weston family left in Duxbury in the year 1947—Etta, with the married name of Thompson.

Mrs. Thompson was located and interviewed. Yes, she said, she was the sister of Addie. Addie had lived in Duxbury and died in Duxbury in 1938. She had married Ernest H. Bailey, her first cousin, who still lived in Duxbury. No, she had had no children.

With hearts in their mouths the searchers asked the question on which everything turned: "Was this Addie's signature?"

The paper shown to Mrs. Thompson was the 1887 adoption record of the Boston Lying-In Hospital, by which Addie Weston had passed her child to Mrs. Mary O'Donnell for adoption.

It was more than likely, even though they had tracked down the right Addie Weston, that no one would know it or could fill in the information necessary to prove it, for in all probability Addie's experience in Boston had been kept a secret from Duxbury. So tying up the Addie Weston of Duxbury with the Addie Weston of Boston depended on an identification of the signature "Addie Weston" in the Boston Hospital record with the Addie Weston of Duxbury. The hope in this regard was equally qualified by fear, for the young lawyers were mindful of the fact that the signature of "Mrs. Mary O'Donnell" in the adoption paper was not the signature of Mary Theresa O'Donnell, and there was an equal chance that the signature of "Addie Weston" might not be genuine. They stood by nervously and anxiously as Mrs. Thompson studied the paper.

After what seemed an interminable length of time the lady replied, "I really wouldn't know."

"Do you have any specimens of her writing that we can use for comparison?" they asked.

Mrs. Thompson thought, then went to a cupboard, and down on her knees she pulled from a neatly stored pile of books a broad, flat book between cardboard covers. The binding had disintegrated and the cover design and lettering had faded. But the title could still be made out—*Warren's Brief Course in*

Geography. It had been published in 1874. This book, Mrs. Thompson explained, had been a schoolbook of Addie's and had been given to the Thompson children fifty years ago. She was sure that Addie's signature was in the book.

The three looked it through. There was a lot of writing, most of it scrawled, inside the cover and on the flyleaf. In one corner, however, was the prim signature "Addie B. Weston, Duxbury, Mass."

The "B," Mrs. Thompson informed her callers, stood for "Bailey," the family name of her mother, the same as the name of the cousin whom Addie had married.

The book was carefully examined for other writing, and there was found, loose inside, a printed sheet of "Rules and Regulations to be observed by the Pupils of Partridge Academy." This also bore a signature of Addie Weston.

A quick comparison of these signatures with the one of Addie Weston in the Boston hospital record satisfied the keen eyes of the lawyers that all three signatures were written by the same hand, although the later one was the mature writing of a woman, while the earlier ones were those of a child. The attorneys presumed that in moving the documents into court they would have to go through an elaborate rigmarole with handwriting experts, but they were confident that they had done their job, performed the miracle and were entitled to whatever decoration could be awarded for a mission accomplished in the field of legal reconnaissance.

Ernest H. Bailey was interviewed the same day, and with him also luck held. He produced a book of Addie's which had been in his home ever since he married her in 1898.

The Life and Times of Wendell Phillips by George L. Austin was well preserved. The 431 pages edged with gold leaf were firmly bound between the ornately decorated covers. The fly-leaf contained a fine Spencerian signature: "Addie B. Weston—September, 1884." This was close to the 1887 date of the hospital record. It was written with care as compared with the hurried and probably harassed signature in the hospital record, but the resemblance was apparent and the deliberate flourish of the "A" and "W" was unmistakably although unconsciously repeated in the 1887 record.

In late July of the court year 1947, the evidence of Etta Thompson and Ernest Bailey was formally recorded in question-and-answer form before a notary public in Duxbury. The record thus made, duly authenticated in legal style, was submitted to the Surrogate when court reconvened on August 11.

At that time the handwriting experts were called in. They had, in the meantime, examined all the signatures of "Addie Weston" and, as is their practice, had blown them up by photographic process into large-size specimens for purposes of illustration and discussion. With these enlargements spread out, they dwelt long and meticulously on the changing styles of writing, similarities and differences in upstrokes and down-strokes, in beginnings and endings of words, in the closing of O's and crossing of T's.

When the scientific and expert testimony was finished there was little doubt that, despite some change in the character of the writing over the years, the same person who had written in the geography book and in *The Life and Times of Wendell Phillips* had signed the record of the Lying-In Hospital, and that that person was Addie Bailey Weston, daughter of William E. and Jerusha Weston of Duxbury. By other records, Addie Weston was shown to have been born in Boston

Signature from
Adoption Record, March 8, 1887

Signature from
Warren's *A Brief Course in Geography*

Signature from
Rules and Regulations for pupils of Partridge Academy

Signature from
Life and Times of Wendell Phillips

Comparison of Addie Weston's Signatures

on December 24, 1863, and to have died in Duxbury on May 28, 1938.

Friedman maintained a front of evincing no interest in the proceedings. He now had to concede that there was a real person answering to the name of Addie Weston and that she was not Mrs. Greer. But he still suggested that Addie Weston was only a blind for the real mother of the child, and in this contention he got some support from Mrs. Thompson and Mr. Bailey.

Mrs. Thompson testified for him that Addie had lived with the family in Duxbury in 1887 and had presented no appearance of being pregnant to her sister, who was then fifteen. "Not at all," said Mrs. Thompson. "I can say that I never knew anything about this thing until it just came out of the clear sky, when these two gentlemen called upon me last week."

Mr. Bailey testified that "all this came as a thunderbolt". He had considered his former wife a virgin when he married her in 1898.

One could not help but reflect, as one heard this testimony, on the strange oblique course a case can take, going so far back into a dead past, suddenly involving people never dreaming that they could have the remotest connection with it in any way, shattering lifelong confidences and laying bare secrets never shared with anyone.

Ernest H. Bailey, solid New England gentleman, wholly innocent, was not even a bystander in the Greer case. But he was caught up in its trail. Because Mabel Seymour on her deathbed had divulged to her lawyer the secret she had kept from her husband for forty years, the secret of Addie Weston, likewise kept from her husband for forty years, had erupted and echoed about him ten years after her death.

What did he think and feel—imposed on, betrayed? Or did

M   [165]

he cling to a cherished belief and accept Friedman's suggestion that there was some other explanation for the appearance of Addie Weston's name in the Boston Hospital record?

Here was a vignette of drama all its own, although only an incident in the sweep of the main drama. So incidental, indeed, that Friedman did not pause to give it thought, but pressed on with the insistent train of his own thought and argument—that Harold Segur was not the child born in the Boston Lying-In Hospital in 1887, but had been born on February 16, 1888, in a place and of a parentage unaccounted for except by Mrs. Greer's description of her child—and by the testimony of one more witness, whom Friedman held in reserve and who, he hoped, in the final hour would tip the scales in his client's favour.

26

Judge Schoonmaker—Proof of
Parentage

*   *   *   *   *

THE man who took the witness stand had thin white hair, a long face strongly lined with the years, eyes soft with remembrance. He sat erect in the witness chair, despite the seventy-nine years he answered for, and he spoke with the voice of a benediction.

John H. Schoonmaker had lived in Ware, Massachusetts, all his life. He had practised law in Ware since his admission to the bar in 1894, and had served a term as the local judge. He had known Dr. Segur all the years that the doctor lived and practised medicine in Ware and before that when the doctor had lived in Enfield, the next town, seven miles away. And he had acted as Dr. Segur's attorney whenever the doctor required legal services.

"Can you recall now, Judge, the matters in which you represented Dr. Segur?" Friedman asked.

"Why, the first work I did for him," the judge recalled, "was collecting some accounts, and then later on other business matters came up and I advised him. There was the matter of his divorce in 1906, and finally the matter of his will, which I drew for him during his last sickness."

"Now, at or prior to the time of the divorce action brought by Dr. Segur against Mary T. Segur, did Dr. Segur speak to you concerning his family?" the lawyer inquired.

"He spoke of a boy called Harry Segur, whom he had adopted some years before," the witness answered.

"Did Dr. Segur ever tell you who the real father of Harold or Harry Segur was?"

Eyes from all sides of the courtroom were fixed on the witness, and in the hush of expectancy ears were intent on the answer.

"He told me he was the father."

The hush was broken and ears strained even more eagerly with the next question.

"Did he say who was the mother of Harry Segur?"

"He said a young woman whom he had got in trouble."

"Is that all he said?"

"That was all."

"Did he state the year?"

"No."

"Did he state the place?"

"Yes, he stated the place—Boston."

Much cross-examination followed, but all it brought out was that until recent inquiry was made of him, the witness had never told anyone of this conversation with Dr. Segur, not even his son with whom he had been practising law for many years.

Thus the trial ended, with wonderment on the part of Wells and Cox and high hopes on the part of Friedman. All awaited the final say of the judge.

27

Decision

*   *   *   *   *

THE trial judge carries a heavy responsibility, especially when he alone must decide the case on the facts as well as on the law. His responsibility is eased considerably when he has a jury of twelve good men and true who become the judges of the facts—when he need only rule on the admissibility of evidence and on points of law and instruct the jury in the applicable law to guide their deliberations.

However difficult it may be at times to state the law, this difficulty is less of a strain and worry than deciding, between all the conflicting evidence, where the truth in fact lies.

Take the simplest kind of case, an automobile accident. The witnesses testify to events which they saw—the same events. Yet the widest discrepancy usually exists between them as to whether the light was red or green, whether a car was on the right or wrong side of the road, how fast it was going and how the accident happened.

There are faults in observation and failings in memory. There are honest mistakes and outright falsehoods. Who is telling the truth? Whose powers of observation and recollection can be trusted? What discount should be made of certain testimony in consideration of the witness's interest in the outcome of the case?

No standard of judgment can be called on to decide these questions other than the elastic one of experience. One cannot go into the library, as the judge can usually do about the law, and look up the answers. That is why the common denominator of the experience of a jury is valuable and comfortable in determining the facts.

The Greer case was far from a simple matter. It was extremely complicated, and the judge was left alone to fathom the truth. Not only were there many witnesses expressing varying versions or opinions with respect to the facts, but in many instances what they testified to had happened so long ago that there were serious questions of how well or accurately they remembered. And there were conflicts in the testimony which could not be explained as honest differences in hearing, understanding or recalling. In some instances someone was not telling the truth. A judge most keenly feels his responsibility when he must determine credibility as between witnesses. Then he yearns for a jury to assume and divide the responsibility.

It is of little solace to the trial judge that a higher court will review the record and his decision. Errors that he may make on the law are readily enough corrected in this way. But an appellate court is at such a disadvantage in reviewing a case on the facts from the printed record, as compared with the trial judge who lived with the trial and heard and observed the witnesses in the flesh, that it is reluctant to interfere with the factual findings of the trial judge and will not do so unless it thinks that he was quite clearly wrong.

Two conflicting stories may look equally plausible in the

record. One or the other may not sound true when actually heard. Not merely what a witness says but how he says it is important. His manner in testifying, the look in his eye, the expression on his face, his hesitancy or forthrightness—these are things which a trial judge or jury can observe and weigh in determining whether to accept, reject or discount a witness's testimony.

It was in the heat of August and after the sweat of counsel had amassed a record of 1,500 pages of testimony and a heap of exhibits that the trial of the Greer case was concluded. It was in the cold of December that Surrogate Delehanty handed down his decision. In the meantime, the attorneys had prepared and exchanged briefs and reply briefs, marshalling their arguments, meeting the opposing arguments, summarizing, explaining, reconciling, emphasizing and discounting the evidence to make it all add up to the sum total each side wanted the judge to find.

And in the meantime, and amidst the trial and consideration of other cases and matters, the learned, conscientious and careful Surrogate pored over the written record, refreshing his recollection of the testimony, considering the arguments of the attorneys and, aided by his keen observation of the witnesses when they were before him, weighing the evidence.

Was Harold Segur the child born in the Boston Lying-In Hospital on February 26, 1887, or could the baby picture and the family observance of his birthday on February 16 be accepted as establishing his birth on February 16, 1888?

Was Mrs. Greer of an age that made possible her giving birth to a child in 1887 or 1888? The records of her own statements of her age, all made during womanhood, indicated the impossibility of such a birth. But, as responsible witnesses suggested, had she been much older than she purported to be? She had generally stated that the father, Willard B. Segur, was a premedical student at the time of the birth of her child. That fact would confirm a birth date at least prior to 1889, when Dr. Segur was graduated from college.

Had Mrs. Greer learned prior to 1939, when she read of the death of Dr. Segur and of his leaving an adopted son, that her child had been adopted by Dr. Segur? Did she know whereof she spoke when she said that Dr. Segur had adopted the child?

What weight was to be given to her contradictory statements, at one time that only Dr. Segur and the Irish lady were present at the birth of the child, and at another time that Drs. Cushing and Derby brought the baby into the world?

Could it be that Harold Segur was the child of Dr. Segur and yet was not the child of Mrs. Greer?

These were the questions the good judge had to struggle with as, on the scales of his mind, balanced by his experience, he weighed the conflicting evidence to determine the truth.

On December 5, 1947, the decision came down. After stating the issue in the case, the judge noted that the burden of proof was on the claimant, Harold Segur, to establish that he was Mrs. Greer's son.

With respect to that burden, he stated: "In an effort to discharge that obligation, claimant has offered declarations of Mrs. Greer respecting the birth to her of an illegitimate child and has sought to identify himself as that child. There is no direct independent evidence to connect him in any way with Mrs. Greer. He never met her or knew of her existence until after she died. It is essential to his case, therefore, that he fit the known facts of his own life history into the description by her of her own child. It is not sufficient that he show some vague similarity between the two. He must show that his history and that of her child depict one and the same person and that he is in fact the child of Mrs. Greer."

Dealing with the evidence, the judge observed: "Mrs. Greer appears to have been under an irresistible compulsion to speak of her youthful error. Her confidences to her employees, her friends and her banking and legal representatives have been detailed at length in the record. It is perhaps natural that the reporters of her talk quote her as making at different times statements varying in some details from those she made to other confidants. Since the occurrence she undertook to recount was one in respect of which the details could scarcely have faded from her memory, it must be supposed that the witnesses themselves have failed to recall the real import of what Mrs. Greer said to them.

"We may put aside for the moment any differences in the factual recitals reportedly emanating from her," he continued, "for there is one matter in respect of which the stories of all witnesses who spoke of her confidences are consistent. She consistently said that her child was born in a house which she characterized either as a boarding house or a private nursing home. She consistently said that she left the child with the woman in charge of the house and that she never saw the child again from the time she herself was able to leave the house."

Taking up then the date and place of birth of Harold Segur, the judge wrote: "Harold Segur claims that he was born in Boston on February 16, 1888. In 1901 he was adopted by Dr. Willard B. Segur and his wife whose maiden name was Mary Theresa O'Donnell and who at the time of her marriage to Dr. Segur in 1895 was known as Mary Baker. This couple executed a petition in 1901 in which they said that the child whom they were adopting was born at the Boston Lying-In Hospital on

February 16, 1887. The Lying-In Hospital records disclose that the male child born there on February 26, 1887, to a woman other than Mrs. Greer, was the only male child born in the hospital in the month of February in the years 1887 or 1888 and taken directly from the hospital for adoption. Such records show that this particular child was the only male child born in the Lying-In Hospital on either February 16 or February 26 in such years. Such records show that the male child born there on February 26, 1887, was removed from the hospital ten . days later when the mother executed her consent to the taking of the child for adoption by 'Mrs. Mary O'Donnell'. The witness to this consent was a Dr. Cliff, who is shown by other testimony to have treated claimant while he lived with Mary Theresa O'Donnell Baker, who eventually married Dr. Segur. The writing of the mother, one Addie Weston, and the opinions respecting such writings which are in the record, satisfy the court that she in fact signed the adoption papers found in the records of the Boston Lying-In Hospital."

While noting that the signature "Mrs. Mary O'Donnell" on the same paper was not in the handwriting of the adopting mother, the judge found that there was enough otherwise in the record to make it clear that Mrs. Willard B. Segur, when she was Mary Theresa O'Donnell or Baker, had obtained a child from Boston Lying-In Hospital and that she had had the assistance of Dr. Cliff in getting the child from the hospital.

"In other words," he said in conclusion on this point, "so far as this record contains affirmative proof as to Harold Segur's origin, it identifies him as the child born in 1887, at the Boston Lying-In Hospital, to a woman concededly not Mrs. Greer."

Delving into Mrs. Greer's declarations concerning the adoption of her child by Dr. Segur and Harold Segur's reliance on those declarations, the Surrogate said: "His case rests principally upon declarations of Mrs. Greer that her child was adopted by Willard B. Segur and had been brought up by him. Since it is shown that he is the only child adopted and reared by Dr. Segur it becomes pertinent to consider what, if any, weight is to be given to the declarations of Mrs. Greer.

"Mrs. Greer consistently said that she had never seen the father of her child or the child himself from the time she left him at the boarding house. Her statements as to the child's adoption and rearing thereafter must, therefore, have been based upon hearsay and not upon her own knowledge, nor upon direct statements to her by the child's father. There is no suggestion as to how she could have received any oral information about her child. The genesis of her statements is revealed in the testimony of her maid. This indicates very clearly that Mrs. Greer had drawn a hasty inference from the news accounts of Dr. Segur's death, which said that he left an adopted son surviving him. Her declarations as to the identity of her child are shown to be based wholly on supposition or speculation on her part."

The matter of Mrs. Greer's age, which loomed so large in the case, was quite briefly disposed of by the court on the basis of the records, which to his mind were not sufficiently contradicted by other evidence.

"The documents in evidence which relate specifically to Mrs. Greer would require a finding that her birth date was in 1881 or later. If her declarations are to be believed it was physically impossible that claimant could have been her son. It is suggested that she minimized her age. Perhaps she did, but nothing in the proof respecting her own declarations about her age can aid him."

Mrs. Sheppard, of course, could not have been believed, or the court could not have reached the decision it did. The judge did not neglect her testimony, however. He met it head on with plain speaking.

"In respect of one of the witnesses produced by claimant some special comment is necessary," he said. "The presence at the trial of this witness illustrates the well-known fact that wide publicity of cases which have in them elements which stir public interest almost always produces a crop of so-called 'witnesses' who have become deluded into the belief that matters which they read about in public prints are matters with which they have had some personal contact. The witness Sheppard falls into that category. The court is satisfied from the content of the testimony of this witness and its own observation of her that she had no knowledge of Mrs. Greer and no contact with her. What she undertook to say is wholly without substance and without weight."

The ultimate conclusion was reached and stated that Harold Segur had failed to establish that he was the son of Mabel Seymour Greer.

Thus ended the Greer case—or so thought all who read the Surrogate's opinion that day.

There would still be a will contest of the conventional kind. Cox, representing the Public Administrator, had won the right to make that contest. It would turn on a simple issue of whether Mrs. Greer had had the mental competency at the time she made the will to know and understand what she was doing.

In that case Wells and Cox would not be sharing the same side of the counsel table. It would be Wells's and Armbruster's responsibility to sustain the will and defend it from attack. In the forthcoming contest Wells and Cox would battle each other as conscientiously and persistently as they had battled together to resist Harold Segur's claim.

All the doctors and nurses who had been in attendance on Mrs. Greer at the end of her life would be called as witnesses, as well as all other persons who saw her during her last days, and, of course, Armbruster. The treatment she received, the amount of sedation, what she said, how she acted—all would be gone into in the minutest detail, for the court to decide whether she had been rational and possessed of her faculties at the time of making her will, or whether she had been so weak of mind and body as to be incompetent in the eyes of the law.

But all this would be a rather uninteresting aftermath as compared with the issue which had so absorbed the court and the public and which had been resolved by the court that day. For all those who had occupied the available seats in the courtroom throughout the trial or followed its progress in the daily Press, the curtain had gone down. Not one, not even the lawyers, thought there would be another act in that drama.

28

Obituary

* * * * *

JOSEPH A. COX was sitting at his desk reading the obituary columns. It was a fine September day and he felt both refreshed and relaxed after a vacation following the conclusion of the trial of the Greer case only a month before. Reading the obituary columns was not really indicative of his thoughts at all. They were back in the Gaspe country on that last flashing fish he had pulled from the sparkling water.

Glancing at the death notices was simply a professional routine for Mr. Cox. He did it almost without thinking and certainly without sentiment. He made his living by representing the estates of persons who died without leaving known relatives. Mr. Cox thus had a lively interest in the dead. The obituary notices in the morning papers were suggestive of possibilities and had become for him an early-morning reading habit.

He was much too busy and his office too well organized, however, to take it on himself to find professional opportunities in this way. The office, as a matter of course, received official reports of all deaths and estate proceedings, and it was a matter of clerical routine to ascertain whether the Public Administrator might assert an interest. Therefore Mr. Cox merely scanned the death notices and received through channels the intelligence on which he relied.

The Greer case was not on his mind this morning—at least not in the forefront. He still had some briefing to do on it for the court, but as an active trial matter it was closed, and closed with the confidence that the judge would have to agree with him that Harold Segur had failed to prove himself to be the son of Mrs. Greer. Who the son was and whether he was dead or alive would probably never be known. The case would always remain the most interesting and perplexing of his career, but tantalizing as the unsolved riddle was, it had to give way to more mundane things. The file had been closed, therefore, with the only precaution which could be taken to catch anything which might yet turn up.

The day Cox finished the trial, he called in his young assistant, Eli Karban, who had been so helpful in connection with the research on the case and in tracking down Addie Weston, and commented, "I am satisfied that Harold Segur is not the son and that the judge will so find. But we have no more idea than when we started who is. He may be dead. May have been dead for years. He may be in Timbuktu. May be in Boston still or possibly in New York. We can't find him alive—no leads. But as you go over the incoming death reports, just keep an eye out for a Segur or Seymour, and if anything turns up let me know.

"And, for good measure," Cox added, "ask one of the public administrators in Boston to give you a flash on any deaths there of a Segur or Seymour. The chance is a long one, but it's the only one left."

This had all gone out of Cox's mind when his morning

[179]

reading was rudely interrupted. The young lawyer bursting in on him had not even bothered to knock.

"Chief," he shrieked, "what do you think of this—a death in Boston on August nineteenth of a man named Seymour, age fifty-three. And guess what's his first name—Willard!"

Cox jumped up like a shot. "Eli, you're not kidding? Any more details?"

"No, sir, but it sure bears looking into."

"It sure does," Cox agreed.

Forgotten for the rest of the day were the mundane things. On the Merchants' Limited at five o'clock Joseph A. Cox was a passenger, on his way to pay a call on a public administrator in Boston.

29

Death in a Hospital

* * * * *

THE alcoholic ward of the Boston City Hospital is not a pretty place. It is not the fresh, clean, antiseptic world of men in white and trim nurses. Nor does the light of hope shine through the distress in the eyes of the patients. The dregs come here, dirty, forlorn. Their eyes, when registering any consciousness, are dull—dulled by drink that has lost its power to relax or revive and only numbs, dulled by life that has turned to despair.

Case histories here are a catalogue of tragedy. And it is usually too late to retrace and find where a life went off the track or lost its moorings. It is always deep in the past—sometimes something physical, always something psychological, a lack of security in self and relations with the outside world, a lack of belonging, an attempt to escape from what one is or isn't to the unreality of the amorphous world of alcohol, the start of the long drift to dereliction.

The doctor who drew the sheet over the unfortunate at 1:30 in the morning of August 19, 1947, wondered where and why this life had gone astray. Medically he recorded: "Immediate cause of death: Cirrhosis of the liver—alcoholism." The admission record told more: Birthplace—Boston. Father—Unknown. Mother—Unknown. Marital history—Single. Children—None. Age—53. Occupation—Carnival worker.

"Hell," muttered the doctor, "the fellow never belonged."

Then he made the closing entry, consignment to a pauper's grave: "Place of burial—Mt. Hope."

30

Mr. Cox Goes to Boston

*   *   *   *   *

COX was cordially received in Boston, not only by the Public Administrator but by the Attorney General of the Commonwealth of Massachusetts. The Commonwealth, through its public officials, was interested in treasure trove, though it be found in potter's field, and Cox was interested in presenting to the court of his own state the true claimant to the treasure. There was a prospective mutual advantage in this unusual comity of states, where the rights lay in one and the pursuit in the other.

Whoever the circus roustabout was who occupied the least regarded bit of Massachusetts earth, he died a citizen of that sovereign state. And if he was born the son of Mabel Seymour, the right he had to contest her will and lay claim to her estate survived and accrued to the state of Massachusetts. It was to the Surrogate's Court of New York, however, that the state of Massachusetts would have to go to assert its claim.

What lay ahead, or more accurately behind, before the claim could be successfully prosecuted, was the vast unknown, the provable perhaps, but the as yet unproved and only surmised.

It would have to be explored, and Cox had definite notions of how to proceed. The Bay State officials who learned that day of Mabel Seymour Greer listened respectfully and with growing enthusiasm to his suggestions.

"The Boston City Hospital record states that he was fifty-three years old," Cox observed in outlining the procedure to be followed in tracking down the origins of the man in whom they were interested. "That would mean that he was born in 1894. First thing to do is to look in the birth records here in Boston to see if there is a record of the birth of this man.

"Then," continued Cox, warming to his subject and calling on his knowledge of Mrs. Greer's habits, "I would suggest that an investigator be sent to the various savings banks in Boston to see if a record can be found of any account of Mabel Seymour around that time."

His listeners looked perplexed.

"You see," he went on, "Mrs. Greer had a penchant for savings-bank accounts. Some of the most valuable information we got about her in New York came from savings-bank records. They revealed birth dates which proved that she couldn't have been the mother of Harold Segur who was born in 1887. My guess is that Mrs. Greer would have opened a savings account wherever she was, and if she lived in Boston at any time I would be surprised if there isn't a savings-bank record to prove it. If we find a birth record of this man Seymour, it is important to show that Mrs. Greer was about Boston at the time when he was born."

The Boston officials readily appreciated the point and agreed to undertake the search.

"Also," added Cox, "court records are good places to look for leads. Mrs. Greer might have brought some proceeding against Dr. Segur for support of the child.

"Many avenues may open up. If the child was abandoned, it is more than likely that he would have come under the care of some state or private charity at some time, and there would be a record made of the child and probably some record of the mother. All these things are worth running down."

Cox left his conferees full of ideas and with quite a chore on their hands. He had not handed them a case on a silver platter. The case might be there—he had blocked out the prospecting—but they would have to do the digging. Only Massachusetts officials can go about the state of Massachusetts, subpoenaing the records of banks and state and private agencies, to see if they can lay claim to a hidden fortune.

31

Willard Seymour

*   *   *   *   *

FROM East Springfield Street to St. Botolph Street in the South End of Boston is only a half-dozen blocks. For the brown-haired, hazel-eyed baby that was born at 16 East Springfield Street, in the shadow of the Boston City Hospital, in May of 1894, to the grey-haired, sullen-eyed man who left his two-dollar-a-week lodging in St. Botolph Street to die in the Boston City Hospital in August 1947, the peregrination was half a century.

He never knew a father. As a small child he knew his mother. He could not remember living with her, although she kept him with her in various rooming houses about Boston for the first year and a half of his life. Then he was boarded out, but she would come and see him or write or send him presents. Whenever she came to see him, it made him feel important. The rest of the time he was acutely conscious of being alone in the world.

Then she disappeared from his life. She came no more; she didn't write. There were no more presents ever. And in later years when he went to work and shifted jobs, as he frequently did, and had to fill out the employment application forms, he always winced at the questions: Mother's name? Father's name? The blanks always had to be filled in "Unknown".

It could not be said that he never had a chance. He was always housed and fed and clothed, and there were those, many of them, who took an interest in him. Mrs. Mary Colson took him into her Dorchester home when he was two years old and gave him care far beyond her bargain. His mother had agreed to pay her three dollars a week for support of the child, but the payments stopped after two years. The mother moved to Philadelphia, where she lived at various addresses under the name of Everett. She wrote Mrs. Colson many promises of payment, but only fifteen dollars were paid over the next three years, and the board bill ran up to five hundred dollars before Mrs. Colson's patience and charity were exhausted.

Then the boy had his first encounter with the law. It was benign. Mrs. Colson had gone to the Society for the Prevention of Cruelty to Children and the Society had gone to court to have the boy declared a neglected child and committed to the State Board of Charity. The mother was not unmindful of the proceeding. She wrote Mrs. Colson asking for more time and advising that she was applying to the Philadelphia Children's Aid Society for help. She even said that she was consulting a lawyer, and on the eve of the court proceeding Mrs. Colson received a telegram over the name of a Philadelphia lawyer asking for a stay of the proceeding. But the judge said that he couldn't tell whether the telegram was genuine and that after such a long period of neglect there was no justification in putting off further the state's taking custodial care of the child.

The care was good and extended over the next eight years, or until the boy was sixteen. At all times he was in a good home and good school. He was originally described as "a fine boy who has had good breeding and training. Attractive but not very rugged-looking. Gets on nicely with other boys and is very happy in new home, enjoying country life." It was recorded in December 1902 that his mother wrote from Philadelphia inquiring about the child.

The entries in the long running record of the state board's custody of the child continued for a while to note that the boy remained good and well and that he was doing well at home and school. But in another year the reporting was of quite a different character. The boy had turned rather sickly and was not doing well at home or at school. When he was ten it was recorded: "He is not as good a boy as he used to be. Has stolen small articles and shows a mean disposition in many ways. Does not get on well with the other boys and it may be well to relocate him where he will be alone."

His place of board was changed. He went to live in a home which had been Whittier's birthplace and slept in a room which Whittier had occupied as a boy. The historical surroundings seemed to interest him, but he was troublesome at school.

His mother came to see him in June 1905 and in the fall wrote to him from a New York City address. At Christmas she sent him some nice presents. That was the last that was heard from her.

The year 1906 seemed to usher in the ill for the boy. He was then twelve. His behaviour went from bad to worse. There was a succession of changes in his living arrangements because no one wanted to keep him. His school work deteriorated, but he finished grade school and was given a chance at higher education at the Governor Dummer Academy. From this institution he was expelled before the end of the first term with the remark: "Should have entered a jail."

He did enter a jail seven years later. It was not a crime of violence or even of meanness. It was a crime of weakness, a yielding to the pressure of poverty, a petty theft from his employer.

Then he changed his name, a break with the past, a past without any anchor, without anything worth remembering, a past one would like to forget and be born again with some identity. William B. Smith was born a man of his own creation.

But neither the world nor his ability to cope with it changed. He never stole again. He worked. He worked as an expressman, a boilermaker's helper, an attendant at a state hospital, a cook at CCC camps, a WPA labourer, and in 1940, when he was laid off, he reached St. Botolph Street and his two-dollar-a-week basement room, for which he could not even pay the rent. William B. Smith had come to his end. The forms which the Public Welfare Department required one to fill out for home relief called for a personal-history statement. Willard Seymour returned to the world of public charity.

He had one job after that, for a while, as a labourer at the Boston Port of Embarkation. He couldn't hold the job, but he continued to live at St. Botolph Street. Only odd jobs as a carnival worker and circus roustabout were available thereafter. His only asset was a Social Security number, which also served as an identification tag.

He became sick as well as alcoholic. On July 30, 1947, he had to go to the hospital. That was the day a coterie of lawyers gathered in the neighbouring town of Duxbury to document the life of Addie Weston and rule out Harold Segur as the heir to half a million dollars.

* 32 *

Pieces of the Puzzle

* * * * *

MR. COX liked jigsaw puzzles. The more pieces and the more intricate the design the better he liked them. Although they were a form of relaxation, he often thought how much they were like some of the law cases he worked on. And on a particular January day in the year 1948, as he was putting together some pieces of evidence in the newfound Greer case, he thought how much like a jigsaw puzzle this case was.

Standing at the large table across the room from his desk, he looked down on the assortment of pieces—reports, letters, records and photostats—that in neat array spread over the table, and he rubbed his hands with satisfaction. They represented the accumulation of information collected over the past several months in Boston, Philadelphia and New York.

"A Tale of Three Cities," he said to himself. "That is the title of this picture, and the pieces fit."

They didn't fit so perfectly but that Wells would find fault and argue that they didn't add up. Cox knew that. But they fitted so well that he was satisfied with the months' work that had brought them together, and he was ready to move them into court for the Surrogate to decide whether they added up to showing Willard Seymour, the late but unlamented roustabout, to be the son of Mabel Seymour Greer.

"Get Mr. Wells on the phone for me, please," he said to his secretary.

The connection made, Cox said in banter, "Frank, do you remember the Greer case—you know, the woman who had a son?"

Laughingly Wells replied, "I have been glad to forget it for some time in getting other work done. Haven't you forgotten it, or don't you have anything else to do in that office of yours?"

"Oh, I have plenty to do," Cox rejoined, "but nothing as interesting as the Greer case. And I just thought that you might be interested in learning that I have found the son!"

There was a definitely speechless moment at the other end of the line before a recovered voice said, "Here we go again." Even then the humour was halfhearted, for Wells knew that Cox was not speaking in jest.

"Yes, Frank, here we go again," Cox assured him, "but this is the real thing. Wouldn't you like to have a look at my collection of documents which prove it, before I show them to the judge? You might be convinced, and I have no secrets from you, although you haven't been my partner in the recent research I have been making."

Wells said that he would be glad to look, although he wasn't glad at all, and an appointment was made for the next day.

Wells was cordially greeted by Cox. They had become good friends through their association in the Greer case and had developed a personal liking as well as a professional regard for each other. Some genuine pleasantry preceded their settling down to business. Then Cox told his visitor of receiving the report of the death of a Willard Seymour—pronouncement of the name made the expected impact on Wells—and of going to Boston and setting in motion the search culminating in the assortment of documents on the near-by table.

"That was last September," he said. "The man died in August —think of the irony of it—just one week after we finished the trial. Since then the Attorney General of Massachusetts and my office have been quite busy documenting the man's life and identifying him as Mrs. Greer's son. It was quite a task, as you might imagine, but we were lucky, and have established his identity beyond a doubt. Let me show you."

Leading Wells over to the table, he said, "Now, Frank, behold the perfect case—all documentary and foolproof. No witness needed to prove a thing. Nobody to examine or cross-examine. No foibles or frailties of witnesses to risk or put up with. The unimpeachable documents tell the incontrovertible story."

Cox beamed like a scientist revealing a highly prized discovery. Wells just looked sceptical.

"You see," Cox continued, "the Boston City Hospital record stated that the man was fifty-three years old. That was the first lead toward establishing his identity. We then went after a corresponding birth record and found it. Here it is, my Exhibit 1, and it all but proves the case by itself." Cox picked up an ancient record from the Boston City Registrar, and, handling it like a rare ingredient in a formula, showed it to Wells.

Its significance was beyond denial—the certificate of a birth, made by one George E. Thompson, M.D., of a male child named Willard Blossom Segur, Jr., born at 16 East Springfield Street, Boston, on May 27, 1894, to Willard Blossom Segur, a physi-

[Under provisions of Chap. 28 of Acts of 1889.]

Return of a Birth to the City Registrar.

Office: Old Court House, Court Square, Boston.

Date of Birth, May 2 1894

Surname of Child, } Willard *Blossom* Segur Jr.
Christian name, if any, }

Sex, Male

White or ~~Colored.~~ (Strike out one.)

Place of Birth, } 16 E. Springfield St.
Street and number, }

Present Residence } " " " "
of Parents, }

Christian Name } Willard Blossom Segur
of Father, }

Christian Name } Mabel Arevalo (Seymour)
of Mother, }

Occupation of } Physician
the Father, }

Father's Birthplace, Ohio

Mother's Birthplace, Spain

los E. Thompson M. D.

[In giving Birthplaces, try to get Name of Town or City.]

cian, whose birthplace was Ohio, and Mabel Arevalo Seymour, whose birthplace was given as Spain.

"Spain!" Wells pounced on the word. "Mrs. Greer wasn't born in Spain. And the name 'Arevalo' doesn't go with her either."

Examining the document more critically, he added, "The name 'Seymour' isn't in the handwriting of whoever made out the rest of the certificate and appears to have been added at a later time. You say you need no witnesses. Who knows that the name Seymour is genuine?"

"Your observations are keen, Frank," Cox conceded. "You might even have noted more, such as the interlineation of the word 'Blossom' in the name of the child, and the adding of 'Segur' to the name of the father in different handwriting." Cox appeared as exacting as Wells. "No, we don't know who made the entries. No one is available who can identify the writings. But there is more, much more, to connect the lady with this child.

"As for the 'Spain' and 'Arevalo,'" he went on, "they were just adopted by Mrs. Greer. You don't know where she was born for that matter. I certainly never took much stock in that England stuff. You know, she always did use the middle initial 'A,' sometimes turning it into Adel or Adele. Why not Arevalo also? You will soon see how free and fancy she was about adopting names. And don't forget Polly Ernest."

Taking the birth certificate back from Wells and returning it to its allotted place on the table, Cox said, "I wanted to be able to show for sure that Mabel Seymour was in Boston in 1894, and I played a hunch that we could find some savings-bank record to prove it. The Attorney General's office in Boston certainly did a fine job at checking and in time came up with these pretty documents. You will admit that is Mrs. Greer's signature, and note the further liberty taken with her name. Perhaps that is the Spanish touch also."

He displayed for Wells's scrutiny a sheet from the Signature Book of the Boston Five-Cent Savings Bank, dated February 12, 1894. In this book all new depositors were required to sign their names and supply certain information. There appeared the signature "Mabelle A. Seymour," undoubtedly in the handwriting of Mrs. Greer, giving her residence as 2 E. Brookline Street, her occupation as nurse, her place of birth England, and her age twenty-one.

Cox also handed over a transcript of the Mabelle A. Seymour account, opened on February 12, 1894, with a deposit of $12.50. It indeed told a short and sad financial story—a withdrawal the next day of $6 and four days later of another $6, leaving a balance of fifty cents. The balance was withdrawn on March 27.

Wells could not question these documents or that they established that Mrs. Greer had been in Boston just prior to the birth of the child Willard Blossom Segur, Jr., on May 27, 1894.

"You note the birthplace is England," he observed, "and if the age there given is correct she was born in 1873."

"Yes," commented Cox, "that is something which will interest Friedman. It's likely that we were wrong and he was right on the matter of age at the trial."

Without further pause, he took from the table a manila envelope, the kind in which lawyers are accustomed to keep legal papers, and, unwinding the cord about it, he said, "A moment ago you questioned the genuineness of the name 'Seymour' on the birth certificate. Now, look at these papers and tell me if you can any longer doubt that Mabel Seymour was the mother of the child. You probably have had no experience in your practice, Frank, with bastardy proceedings, or paternity proceedings as we now call them. They are quite common, however, and it happened that Mabel A. Seymour brought a proceeding against Dr. Segur to have him adjudged the father of her child. These are the court papers."

Wells looked them through—a complaint in the name of Mabel A. Seymour, and a summons of the Boston court, both dated September 19, 1894, charging Willard B. Segur with being the father of Mabel Seymour's child born on May 28, 1894.

"But there is no signature of Mabel Seymour here to establish her identity," he pointed out hopefully.

"No, no signature," mused Cox. "They evidently didn't make the parties verify their pleadings in those days. But it leaves you very little to go on. This is more than coincidence that a Mabel Seymour claimed that Willard Segur was the father of her child, born at the time stated in the birth certificate you have seen, and you know there were not two Mabel Seymours claiming that Dr. Segur was the father of their child."

"Let us suppose you are right as to the birth of a child to Mabel Seymour in May 1894," Wells countered. "Still you haven't established that the man Willard Seymour who died in the Boston City Hospital in 1947 was the child of Mabel Seymour born in 1894."

"One step at a time," counseled Cox. "I'm not through. There is a lot more."

He then proceeded to march out the other documents which covered the table.

First, an application dated May 23, 1895, made by Mabel A. Seymour, also described as Mabelle A. Seymour, age 23, born in Canada, to the Overseers of the Poor in the City of Boston, for support of her child, William A. Segur. The birth date of the child was given as May 22, 1894, and the name of the father as William B. Segur, a physician, born in Ohio.

Second, records of Gwynne Temporary Home for Children, a private charity in Boston, showing that a child Willard Blossom Segur, Jr., born in Boston on May 28, 1894, son of Mabelle Seymour, was taken by the Home on December 18, 1895, and returned to his mother on May 16, 1896. The mother was described in the records as being a nurse and as having been born in Madrid, Spain.

This was followed by the long record of the Massachusetts State Board of Charity, running from 1902 to 1910, accounting for its custody of "Willard B. Seymour, born May 28, 1894, child of Willard B. Segur and Mabel A. Seymour." The record made note of the fact that the putative father had denied paternity of the child and that a settlement in bastardy proceedings had been made out of court. Note was also made of all communications received from the mother, whether under the name Mabel Seymour from New York or Mary Everett from Philadelphia. The communications from Philadelphia came from 1203 Locust Street.

Finishing his perusal of these documents, Wells remarked, "This record ends in 1910. I still don't see that you have connected the ward of the State Board of Charity, assuming that he was the son of Mrs. Greer, with the Willard Seymour who died thirty-seven years later."

"There will be no missing link," Cox assured him. "We don't have daily or yearly records thereafter, but Seymour shows up at sufficient intervals, and each appearance is connected with the same person.

"Take this 'Personal History Statement of Willard Seymour' that he made out in 1942 to get a job as a patrolman at the

Boston Port of Embarkation." Cox held up a governmental form with its detailed set of questions.

"Note," he said, "that although he was not able to state at that time who his mother or father was, the telltale birth date is given—May 28, 1894—and under 'Education,' Governor Dummer Academy is listed. So, obviously, it is our man."

Wells studied the form, which stated the address of Seymour at that time as being 16 St. Botolph Street, Boston, and listed his changing employment over the years, and his Social Security number, 029-8870. The last question on the form was "In case of emergency, notify——." He had written in "No one to notify."

"And then?" asked Wells.

"Then the end. And that it was the same Willard Seymour is proved three ways," Cox replied. "Here, look at the record of his admission to the Boston City Hospital on July 30, 1947, and the death certificate."

Wells observed the significant statements:

Address—16 St. Botolph Street.

Education—Governor Dummer.

Social Security No.—029-8870.

"Full cycle. You couldn't document your own life that well" was Cox's final, proud pronouncement.

"What about the Philadelphia and Everett features?" Wells objected. "Don't they suggest someone other than Mrs. Greer in the picture?"

"Not at all," snapped Cox. "Everett was just another name assumed by the lady, like Ernest and Arevalo. Mrs. Greer may never have gone under the name Seymour in Philadelphia, but she was in Philadelphia all right and used the name Everett. Again a savings-bank account tells the story."

He produced from another folder, occupying its particular

o   [197]

niche on his table, records from the Union Dime Savings Bank in New York. Account No. 376357 was opened on February 23, 1901, by Mabel Seymour. The required signature was unquestionably in the handwriting of Mrs. Greer. She gave her address at the time as 244 West Fifty-first Street, New York City, and her age as twenty-two. The two withdrawal slips, however, by which the $25 deposited in February were withdrawn in March, showed a Philadelphia address, and the cheques were cashed at a Philadelphia bank.

"You will recall," continued Cox, "that the record of the Massachusetts Board of Charity disclosed the address of the mother in Philadelphia, under the name of Mary Everett, as 1203 Locust Street. And here is a tidbit which fills in that part of the picture. Copsill's Philadelphia City Directory for 1903, page 783. See it for yourself." Cox handed over a bulky clothbound volume, with a marker at that page.

Wells read the entry: "Everett, Mary, Boarding, 1203 Locust."

"You haven't overlooked much, have you?" he said with evident appreciation.

"One can't," the other rejoined, "when dealing with a supercritical fellow like you. But it all hangs together."

Wells was afraid that it did, although he was not prepared to concede that much on the spot. He knew that he would look at these documents long and critically to see if he could find any flaws in the chain before he handed over the money at stake.

Without further comment he took his leave. Cox returned to his table and looked admiringly at the picture.

33

Court Reconvenes

* * * * *

LAWSUITS, like politics, can make strange bedfellows. When the Surrogate's Court was reconvened on June 25, 1948, and once more "The Matter of Mabel Seymour Greer" was called, Friedman and Wells were seated on the same side of the counsel table. Cox was on the other side, but he was not alone. He was flanked by the Attorney General of Massachusetts and the Public Administrator from Boston. The Commonwealth was there to claim its own.

The issue, as in the prior trial in reference to Harold Segur, was whether Willard Seymour was the son of Mrs. Greer. If he was proved to be, the state of Massachusetts had the right in his name to contest the will of Mrs. Greer on the ground that she was not competent when she made the will. Then, if successful in establishing that claim, the state would be entitled to receive all her property. Its first burden, however, before it got to the second point, was to establish its claim that the deceased Seymour was Mrs. Greer's son.

The evidence on this claim was placed before the court quickly and smoothly. Cox had removed it in its orderly organization from his table to the courtroom. The showing was as neat and compact before the judge as it had been before Wells a few months back. In the meantime Friedman also had a showing and was ready to join Wells in whatever attack they could make on the documentation.

In fact, Friedman was somewhat more pleased with the prospect than was Wells. The newfound evidence supported his contention as to Mrs. Greer's age. Now he could seize on the Boston Five-Cent Savings Bank record of 1894, when Mabel Seymour said that she was twenty-one, or born in 1873 or perhaps even in 1872, and argue that it was not only possible for her to have given birth to Harold Segur in 1888 but that Segur fitted her description of a child born to her in her "early teens," while the other child was born when she was twenty-one.

Friedman and Wells took turns in impeaching the documents paraded by Cox. They dwelt critically on the birth record—the additions and interlineations, the different handwritings, suggesting an altered document—and vigorously argued that all the record established was that a child was born to a Mabel Arevalo, whose birthplace was Spain and who was not Mrs. Greer. Except for the addition of the name Seymour to the birth certificate—no one knew how much later or by whom or by what authority or on what information—there was nothing, they contended, to indicate any connection between this birth and Mabel Seymour.

The court docket of the Boston bastardy proceedings, brought by Mabel A. Seymour against Willard B. Segur, did not establish the identity of the mother, they argued, because there was no identifying signature in the papers.

As for the detailed record of the life of Willard Seymour,

they pointed out that it was at variance with Mrs. Greer's descriptions of her child. Quite an array of variances was made out:

Mrs. Greer had consistently stated that she had never seen or heard from her child since leaving it with an Irishwoman. No Irishwoman appeared in the life of Willard Seymour, and the record showed that his mother had maintained contact with the child over a period of years. Friedman reminded the judge that the Irishwoman went with Harold Segur.

Mrs. Greer had always referred to the father of her child as being a college student, taking premedical courses. When the child of 1894 was born, Dr. Segur had been in practice for two years. Again Friedman pointed out that the description given by Mrs. Greer fitted Harold Segur, who was born at a time when Dr. Segur was in college taking premedical courses.

Mrs. Greer had stated alternately that no doctor was present at the birth of her child and that the doctors who brought her child into the world were Dr. Harvey Cushing and a Dr. Derby, whereas a Dr. Thompson had attended at the birth of the child in 1894.

Of course, there was no adoption of the 1894 child, and Friedman continued to credit Mrs. Greer's statements that her child had been adopted by Dr. Segur.

All in all, both lawyers argued, the Public Administrator had not sustained the burden of proof. The new evidence, as well as the old, was much more consistent with Harold Segur's being the child, Friedman insisted.

"It would be the final irony," he eloquently pleaded, "if this estate should go to the state of Massachusetts on a decision that the child was one who is dead, who could never enjoy a penny of his inheritance, and who died in squalid poverty without even knowing his heritage."

With the same ringing tone with which he had first asserted the claim of Harold Segur, Friedman closed the case.

"Your Honour, I respectfully submit," he said, "that the new evidence brought before you this day, most importantly the evidence of Mrs. Greer's age, reinforces Harold Segur's claim. Only he can qualify as Mrs. Greer's son under the statements of identification made by her. I feel that your Honour ruled against him at the last trial because it appeared that Mrs. Greer was born in 1881 and couldn't have been the mother of a child born in 1888. Now we know that Mrs. Greer was born at least as early as 1873 and certainly could have been the mother of Harold Segur. On the whole case, I beg your Honour to reconsider your former decision against my client and award him his rights, which he is still able to enjoy."

The impassive judge with the slightest nod acknowledged the end of the case. The panelled door behind the bench silently opened as he rose and silently closed behind him.

34

Final Judgment

*   *   *   *   *

O NE month later, in the ebb of another summer, just before the resumption of a new term of court, with its new
estates and fresh contests, the Surrogate pronounced the final
word which a court could pronounce on the "Matter of Mabel
Seymour Greer."

"The prior decision of the court," he wrote, "which eliminated
one Segur as a party to this proceeding, sufficiently outlines the
history of Mrs. Greer's multiple statements concerning the birth
to her of an illegitimate son. The matter now submitted for decision concerns the right of the Public Administrator, as administrator of one Willard Seymour, to assert a claim against Mrs.
Greer's estate. The central question is whether this individual
is the son born to Mabel Seymour Greer.

"The rule respecting the burden of proof resting on a claimant such as the present one is stated in the prior decision. Re-
examination in detail of the whole body of exhibits confirms the
view formed by the court during the hearing that the required
standard of proof has been met.

"There are discrepancies of one sort and another in the record, some arising from the exhibits themselves and some from the variances among the many reports Mrs. Greer gave of her early experience; but the whole is so persuasive as to leave no doubt in the mind of the court that the person who died at Boston City Hospital on August 19, 1947, under the name Willard Seymour, was in truth the son of Mrs. Greer."

35

Post-Mortems

*   ◦   ☙   *   ●

THERE are postscripts and post-mortems to most lawsuits. The case ends, the court closes, but follow the parties to their homes and the lawyers to their offices and you will hear the regrets and recriminations, the convictions and compromises, the rationalizations and reconciliations, and the second guesses. They may echo down the years.

The Greer case was ultimately settled. The trial and decision determined only the issue of heirship. The Commonwealth of Massachusetts became entitled to contest the validity of Mrs. Greer's will and to lay claim to her property. That meant another lawsuit. But there is a long-standing comity between the Commonwealth and its leading educational institution. They did not wish to litigate further the issue between them, and in the end they divided the financial stake.

For Harold Segur the resulting values were purely personal. He still works at the same job which has occupied him for the past twenty years, satisfied, secure and respected, and he still lives in his second-floor apartment on Auburn Street, Worcester, happy in his family and content in his certainty that Dr. Segur was his father.

Lester Friedman, if drawn into conversation, will now concede that Willard Seymour was the son of Mrs. Greer. But he will stoutly maintain that Harold Segur was also her son. He has a theory which fits all the facts. He believes that the liaison between Dr. Segur and Mabel Seymour was of long duration, extending at least from 1887 to 1894, and that Harold Segur was their mutually acknowledged child, while Willard Seymour may not have been the son of Dr. Segur.

"Remember," he will say, "that Dr. Segur denied paternity of the child born in 1894. Mrs. Greer was, therefore, left with sole responsibility for him. How she maintained contact with that child for years and disowned him only as favourable prospects for her life opened up, and were threatened by continued contact with him, is recorded in the case history of the Massachusetts State Board of Charity. This child was put out of heart and mind, lost and forgotten as far as Mrs. Greer was concerned.

"Harold Segur, however, was a child whose whereabouts remained known, in a 'safe place,' as she would say. 'Safe' for her as well as for him. Mary Theresa O'Donnell, the Irish lady, took him at birth and in due course Dr. Segur adopted him. He was anchored, and anchored in Mrs. Greer's memory. He was a child she could identify and in time was willing, even anxious, to identify. Hence everything she said to everybody respecting the identification of her child fits Harold Segur, not Willard Seymour—that he was born when she was sixteen and Dr. Segur was a college student, that he was taken at birth by an Irish lady, that she never saw him again and that he was adopted by his father.

"He was her son and should have been awarded a share in her estate," Friedman will conclude.

"Do you still think the Piping Rock incident was a fabrication of Frank Reitman?" he is sometimes asked.

"I don't know," he will say, "but the real significance of the Piping Rock incident was its impact on Mrs. Greer. She knew that Harold Segur would not put in such an appearance. Her fear was that the other son might turn up and ruin her life."

The Honourable Joseph A. Cox, now a Justice of the Supreme Court of the State of New York, is reflective about the Greer case in a different vein.

"No, Friedman is indulging his imagination," he will say. "He was misled originally, as we all were misled, by Mrs. Greer's statements to her employees and friends, and finally to her attorney. But in the end truth did out, and it was quite different from the picture painted by Mrs. Greer, and it leaves no room for any claim that Harold Segur bore the remotest connection to her. He may have been the son of Dr. Segur, yes, but of Mrs. Greer, no.

"The Greer case was two cases and two Mrs. Greers. The first case was premised on her own representations of herself as reflected and repeated by her friends—a woman ten years younger than she actually was, who as a girl-mother, the victim of inexperience, had been caught in the toils of an illegitimate birth and, overwhelmed by the situation, had abandoned her child of necessity, but not without seeing that he was cared for. All of her statements were excusatory and calculated to enlist the sympathy of those whose favourable opinion she sought. Her prompting and purpose, I believe, were to assure their support in the event that her child should appear on the scene.

"The second trial revealed the unvarnished facts and quite a different Mrs. Greer—a woman who was neither a very young girl nor inexperienced at the time of the birth of her child. She was a nurse. She was smart enough to hale the putative father of her child into court and press him for a settlement. Any professed belief of hers that Dr. Segur adopted her child must be weighed against her knowledge that he had contested the paternity charge and denied responsibility for her pregnancy. She maintained contact with the child for years and completely abandoned him only as her own security dictated.

"The explanation of the contradictions between Mrs. Greer's description of her child and the actual facts is psychological. Her conscience, or at least her explanation of events, was eased by self-justifying alterations of the truth. She felt that her confessions or confidences would be more sympathetically received if the child was made out to be a child of her very young age and a child that was immediately and permanently detached from her in favour of better keeping. She was not willing to admit to others that she had maintained contact with the child for years and turned her back on him only as she approached a better life for herself. Likewise she seized on the late information that Dr. Segur left an adopted son to identify her child with that man because it was what she would have liked to believe and wished others to believe.

"What she said about doctors present at the delivery of the child also illustrates the point. She wasn't willing to tell the truth. So her earliest reported version was that no doctor was present at the birth of the child. When she came to her latest version in reporting to Armbruster, when her mind was slipping badly, she did some grandiose fancifying and called up the name of the famous Dr. Harvey Cushing."

Mr. Justice Cox will also explain that justice was done in the Greer case. "The fortune was not wasted. It was put to good use," he says. "The share taken by the state of Massachusetts was only partial reimbursement for the kind of expense a state is incurring all the time for the custody and care of children like Willard Seymour."

Francis D. Wells permits only a philosophical smile to cross his face when asked about the Greer case. "Very, very interesting" is his only comment. But he did make a sentimental journey to Boston, when the case was completely finished, to suggest that the Commonwealth of Massachusetts give belated recognition to Willard Seymour by placing a marker at his grave.

ABOUT THE AUTHOR

JUSTICE DAVID W. PECK *is Presiding Justice of the Appellate Division of the New York State Supreme Court, First Department, one of the most important courts in the United States. He was born in Crawfordsville, Indiana, educated there at Wabash College (Phi Beta Kappa). He took his law degree at Harvard Law School. Early in his career he was Assistant United States Attorney in New York and for ten years a partner in the law firm of Sullivan and Cromwell. From 1943 to 1945 he was a Justice of the Supreme Court of the State of New York, serving as a trial judge. In 1945 he was designated by the Governor as an Associate Justice of the Appellate Division and in 1947 as Presiding Justice. He lives in New York, is married and has two sons.*